CONTENTS

Targeting Homework
Year 1 New Edition

Copyright © 2023 Blake Education
Reprinted 2024, 2025

ISBN: 978 1 92572 643 5

Published by Pascal Press
PO Box 250
Glebe NSW 2037
www.pascalpress.com.au
contact@pascalpress.com.au

Author: Norah Colvin
Publisher: Lynn Dickinson
Editor: Ruth Schultz
Cover and Text Designer: Leanne Nobilio
Typesetter: Ruth Schultz
Images & Illustrations: Dreamstime (unless otherwise indicated);
p. 56 Sara Dickinson

Printed by Wai Man Book Binding (China) Ltd

Acknowledgements
Thank you to the publishers, authors and illustrators
who generously granted permission for their work
to be reproduced in this book.

Introduction

Targeting Homework aims to build and reinforce English and Maths skills. This book supports the ACARA Australian Curriculum for Year 1 and helps children to revise and consolidate what has been taught in the classroom. ACARA codes are shown on each unit and a chart explaining their content descriptions is on pages v and vi. The inside back cover (Maths) and front cover (English) show the topics in each unit.

The structure of this book

This book has 32 carefully graded double-page units – 16 for English and 16 for Maths.

The English units are divided into three sections:

- ★ Grammar and Punctuation
- ★ Spelling and Phonic Knowledge
- ★ Reading and Comprehension — includes a wide variety of literary and cross-curriculum texts.

This also includes a Reading Review segment for children to record and rate their home reading books and some handwriting practice.

> **My Book Review**
>
> Title _____
>
> Author _____
>
> Colour stars to show your rating: ☆ ☆ ☆ ☆ ☆
>   Boring   Great!
>
> Comment _____
> _____

The Maths units are divided between:

- ★ Number and Algebra
- ★ Measurement and Space
- ★ Statistics
- ★ Problem Solving.

Assessment

Term Reviews follow Units 1–8, 9–16, 17–24 and 25–32 to test work covered during the term, and allow parents and carers to monitor their child's progress. Children are encouraged to mark each unit as it is completed and to colour in the traffic lights at the end of each segment. These results are then transferred to the Marking Grid. Parents and carers can see at a glance if their child is excelling or struggling!

- ● **Green** = Excellent — 2 or fewer questions incorrect
- ● **Orange** = Passing — 50% or more questions answered correctly
- ● **Red** = Struggling — fewer than 50% correct and needs help

SCORE **/18** (0-6) (8-14) (16-18)   *Score 2 points for each correct answer!*

How to Use This Book

The activities in this book are specifically designed to be used at home with minimal resources and support. Helpful explanations of key concepts and skills are provided throughout the book to help understand the tasks. Useful examples of how to do the activities are provided.

Regular practice of key concepts and skills will support the work your child does in school and will enable you to monitor their progress throughout the year. It is recommended that children complete 8 units per school term (one a week) and then the Term Review. Every unit has a Traffic Light scoreboard at the end of each section.

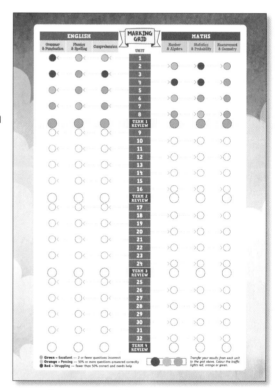

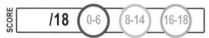

Score 2 points for each correct answer!

You or your child should mark each completed unit and then colour the traffic light that corresponds to the number of correct questions. This process will enable you to see at a glance how your child is progressing and to identify weak spots. The results should be recorded at the end of each term on the Marking Grid on page 1. The Term Review results are important for tracking progress and identifying any improvements in performance. If you find that certain questions are repeatedly causing difficulties and errors, then there is a good reason to discuss this with your child's teacher and arrange for extra instruction in that problem area.

NOTE: The Maths Problem Solving questions do not appear on the Marking Grid as they often have multiple or subjective answers that cannot be easily scored.

Home Reading Journal

Each English unit provides space for your child to log, review and rate a book they have read during the week. These details can then be transferred to the handy Reading Journal Summary on page 146, which can be photocopied and shared with their teacher or kept as a record.

Answers

The answer section on pages 147–162 can be removed, stapled together and kept somewhere safe. Use it to check answers when your child has completed each unit. Encourage your child to colour in the Traffic Light boxes when the answers have been calculated.

TARGETING HOMEWORK 1 © PASCAL PRESS ISBN 9781925726435

Australian Curriculum Correlations: Year 1 English		Grammar & Punctuation	Phonic Knowledge & Spelling	Reading Comprehension
CODE	**CODE DESCRIPTION**	**UNITS**	**UNITS**	**UNITS**
LANGUAGE				
AC9E1LA01	Understand how language, facial expressions and gestures are used to interact with others when asking for and providing information, making offers, exclaiming, requesting and giving commands			27
AC9E1LA06	Understand that a simple sentence consists of a single independent clause representing a single event or idea	1, 3, 5, 7, 9, 11, 13, 25, 29		
AC9E1LA07	Understand that words can represent people, places and things (nouns, including pronouns), happenings and states (verbs), qualities (adjectives) and details such as when, where and how (adverbs)	5, 15, 17, 25, 29, 31		
AC9E1LA08	Compare how images in different types of texts contribute to meaning			3
AC9E1LA10	Understand that written language uses punctuation such as full stops, question marks and exclamation marks, and uses capital letters for familiar proper nouns	1, 3, 5, 7, 9, 11, 13, 15, 17, 19, 21, 23		
LITERATURE				
AC9E1LE04	Listen to and discuss poems, chants, rhymes and songs, and imitate and invent sound patterns including alliteration and rhyme			9, 25
LITERACY				
AC9E1LY01	Discuss different texts and identify some features that indicate their purposes			1, 3, 5, 7, 9, 11, 13, 15, 17, 19, 21, 23, 25, 27, 29, 31
AC9E1LY05	Use comprehension strategies such as visualising, predicting, connecting, summarising and questioning when listening, viewing and reading to build literal and inferred meaning by drawing on vocabulary and growing knowledge of context and text structures			1, 3, 5, 7, 9, 11, 13, 15, 17, 19, 21, 23, 25, 27, 29, 31
AC9E1LY08	Write words using unjoined lower-case and upper-case letters		1, 3, 5, 7, 9, 11, 13, 15, 17, 19, 21, 23, 25, 27, 29, 31	
AC9E1LY09	Segment words into separate phonemes (sounds) including consonant blends or clusters at the beginnings and ends of words (phonological awareness)		1, 3, 5, 7, 9, 11, 13, 15, 17, 19, 21, 23	
AC9E1LY11	Use short vowels, common long vowels, consonant blends and digraphs to write words, and blend these to read one- and two-syllable words		1, 3, 5, 7, 9, 11, 13, 15, 17, 19, 21, 23, 25, 27, 29, 31	
AC9E1LY12	Understand that a letter can represent more than one sound and that a syllable must contain a vowel sound		25, 27	
AC9E1LY13	Spell one- and two-syllable words with common letter patterns		29, 31	
AC9E1LY15	Recognise and know how to use grammatical morphemes to create word families	19, 21, 23, 27		

Australian CURRICULUM

Australian Curriculum Correlations: Year 1 Maths		Number & Algebra	Statistics	Measurement & Space	Problem Solving
CODE	CONTENT DESCRIPTION	UNITS	UNITS	UNITS	UNITS
NUMBER					
AC9M1N01	Recognise, represent and order numbers to at least 120 using physical and virtual materials, numerals, number lines and charts	2, 4, 6, 8, 10, 12, 14, 16, 18, 20, 22, 24, 26, 28, 30, 32			6, 22, 30, 32
AC9M1N02	Partition one- and two-digit numbers in different ways using physical and virtual materials, including partitioning two-digit numbers into tens and ones	14, 20, 22, 24, 26, 28, 30, 32			
AC9M1N03	Quantify sets of objects, to at least 120, by partitioning collections into equal groups using number knowledge and skip counting	2, 6, 8, 10, 12, 16, 20, 22, 32			
AC9M1N04	Add and subtract numbers within 20, using physical and virtual materials, part-part-whole knowledge to 10 and a variety of calculation strategies	2, 4, 6, 8, 10, 12, 14, 16, 18, 20, 22, 24, 26, 28, 30, 32	3		12, 32
AC9M1N05	Use mathematical modelling to solve practical problems involving additive situations including simple money transactions; represent the situations with diagrams, physical and virtual materials, and use calculation strategies to solve the problem	2, 4, 6, 8, 10, 12, 14, 16, 18, 20, 22, 24, 26, 28, 30, 32			8
AC9M1N06	Use mathematical modelling to solve practical problems involving equal sharing and grouping; represent the situations with diagrams, physical and virtual materials, and use calculation strategies to solve the problem	8, 16, 24, 32			
ALGEBRA					
AC9M1A01	Recognise, continue and create pattern sequences, with numbers, symbols, shapes and objects, formed by skip counting, initially by twos, fives and tens	2, 6, 10, 12, 16, 18, 20, 22, 26, 28, 30, 32			
AC9M1A02	Recognise, continue and create repeating patterns with numbers, symbols, shapes and objects, identifying the repeating unit	2, 16, 32			
MEASUREMENT					
AC9M1M01	Compare directly and indirectly and order objects and events using attributes of length, mass, capacity and duration, communicating reasoning			2, 4, 8, 10, 18, 24, 26	2, 18, 26
AC9M1M02	Measure the length of shapes and objects using informal units, recognising that units need to be uniform and used end-to-end			18	10
AC9M1M03	Describe the duration and sequence of events using years, months, weeks, days and hours			12, 20, 28	20
SPACE					
AC9M1SP01	Make, compare and classify familiar shapes; recognise familiar shapes and objects in the environment, identifying the similarities and differences between them			2, 10, 18, 26	2, 14, 24
AC9M1SP02	Give and follow directions to move people and objects to different locations within a space			4, 20, 28	4, 28
STATISTICS					
AC9M1ST01	Acquire and record data for categorical variables in various ways including using digital tools, objects, images, drawings, lists, tally marks and symbols		22, 30		
AC9M1ST02	Represent collected data for a categorical variable using one-to-one displays and digital tools where appropriate; compare the data using frequencies and discuss the findings		6, 14		

AC | Australian CURRICULUM

TARGETING HOMEWORK 1 © PASCAL PRESS ISBN 9781925726435

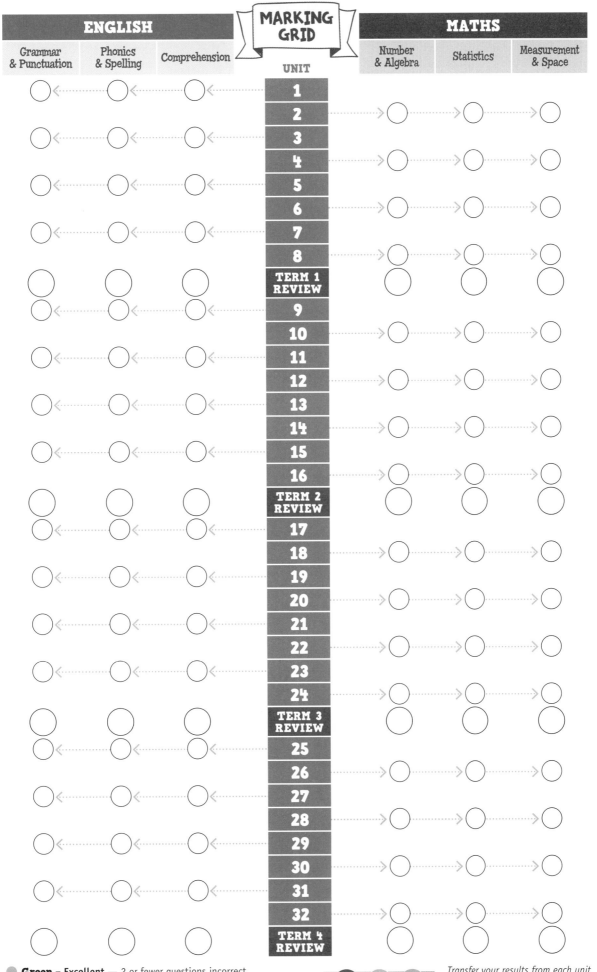

MARKING GRID

ENGLISH

| Grammar & Punctuation | Phonics & Spelling | Comprehension |

MATHS

| Number & Algebra | Statistics | Measurement & Space |

UNIT

1
2
3
4
5
6
7
8
TERM 1 REVIEW
9
10
11
12
13
14
15
16
TERM 2 REVIEW
17
18
19
20
21
22
23
24
TERM 3 REVIEW
25
26
27
28
29
30
31
32
TERM 4 REVIEW

Green = Excellent — 2 or fewer questions incorrect
Orange = Passing — 50% or more questions answered correctly
Red = Struggling — fewer than 50% correct and needs help

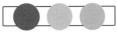

Transfer your results from each unit to the grid above. Colour the traffic lights red, orange or green.

Grammar & Punctuation

AC9E1LA10, AC9E1LA06

What is a sentence?

This is a **sentence**:

   The little bird sat in the nest.

A sentence is a group of words that makes sense on its own.

A sentence begins with a **capital letter** and ends with a **full stop**.

   The little bird sat in the nest.

   ↑capital letter   ↑full stop

This is **not** a sentence: **a little bird**

It is a group of words, but they do not make sense on their own.

Complete these sentences that tell about you.
Circle the capital letters and full stops in the sentences.

①   Hello, my name is _____ .

②   I am a _____ .

③   I am _____ years old.

④   I like to _____ .

⑤   My favourite colour is _____ .

⑥   My favourite food is _____ .

Rewrite these sentences correctly.
Make each sentence begin with a capital letter and end with a full stop.

⑦   the dog ran after the stick

_____

⑧   a book is on the table

_____

⑨   the girl has a pet cat

_____

⑩   a monkey is in the tree

_____

Score 2 points for each correct answer!   **SCORE**   **/20**   10-14

TARGETING HOMEWORK 1 © PASCAL PRESS ISBN 9781925726435

Short vowel sounds

The **short vowel** sounds are **a, e, i, o, u.**

You can hear the short vowel sounds in these words:

bat   **egg**   **pig**   **dog**   **sun**

Write the short vowel to complete these words.

① p___n

② j___m

③ tr___ck

④ z___p

⑤ k___ng

⑥ f___x

⑦ c___t

⑧ n___st

Read these groups of words. Cross out the word that has a different short vowel.

⑨ cat can duck bag

⑩ pig tin big bug

⑪ sun bug jam bus

⑫ leg pig pet egg

⑬ zip dog pot mop

Trace the words. Start at the star. Follow the arrows.

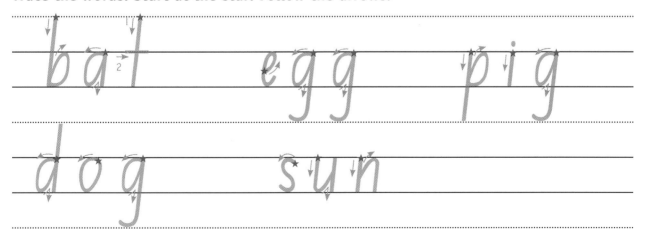

Imaginative text – Narrative

The Billabong

On Sunday, a bullfrog came to the billabong.
"I will live here," he said.

On Monday, two pelicans came to the billabong.
"We will live here," they said.

On Tuesday, three turtles came to the billabong.
"We will live here," they said.

On Wednesday, four crayfish came to the billabong.
"We will live here," they said.

On Thursday, five platypuses came to the billabong.
"We will live here," they said.

On Friday, the bullfrog started to croak. The pelicans began to flap.
The turtles splashed, the crayfish nipped and the platypuses kicked.
It was very noisy at the billabong.

On Saturday, a crocodile came to the billabong.
He wanted to see what all the fuss was about.

On Sunday, it was very quiet at the billabong.
The crocodile lay in the water and smiled.

Reading & Comprehension

Write or tick the correct answers.

① Where does the story take place?

_____

For each day, write who came to the billabong.

② Sunday

_____

③ Monday

_____

④ Tuesday

_____

⑤ Wednesday

_____

⑥ Thursday

_____

⑦ Friday

_____

⑧ Saturday

_____

⑨ Why did the crocodile come to the billabong?

☐ a It wanted a home.

☐ b It heard all the noise.

☐ c It was lonely.

⑩ Why was it quiet at the billabong on Sunday?

☐ a The animals were sleeping.

☐ b The crocodile frightened them away.

☐ c The crocodile ate them.

Score 2 points for each correct answer! | SCORE | /20 | 0-8 | 10-14 | 16-20

My Book Review

Title _____

Author _____

Colour stars to show your rating: ☆ ☆ ☆ ☆ ☆

Boring   Great!

Comment _____

_____

Number & Algebra

AC9M1N01, AC9M1N03, AC9M1N04, AC9M1N05, AC9M1A01, AC9M1A02

Numbers to 20

| 1 | 2 | 3 | 4 | 5 | 6 | 7 | 8 | 9 | 10 | 11 | 12 | 13 | 14 | 15 | 16 | 17 | 18 | 19 | 20 |

Count the objects. Write the number in the box.

① [ ]

③ [ ]

② [ ]

④ [ ]

Write the number that comes next.

⑤ 6, 7, 8, _____

⑥ 12, 13, 14, _____

⑦ 8, 9, 10, _____

Write the missing numbers.

⑧

| | 1 | 2 | 3 | | 5 | 6 | 7 | | | 10 | 11 | 12 |

⑨ 4 5 6 [ ] 8 9 [ ] [ ] [ ]

Skip count in 2s. Write the numbers that come next.

⑩ 2 4 6 8 ____ ____ ____ ____ ____ ____

TERM 1 MATHS

TARGETING HOMEWORK 1 © PASCAL PRESS ISBN 9781925726435

Skip count in **5s.** Write the numbers that come next.

⑪

5

Draw the number of objects in the box.

⑫ 8 circles

⑬ 13 squares

Count the turtles on the dominoes. Write how many turtles **altogether.**

⑭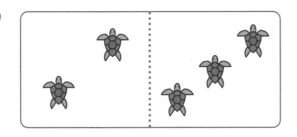

☐ and ☐ makes ☐

⑮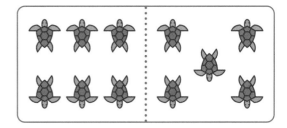

☐ and ☐ makes ☐

Repeating patterns

What comes next? Draw the next shape. Circle the part of the pattern that repeats.

⑯

⑰

⑱

Score 2 points
for each
correct answer!

SCORE

/ 36 0-16 18-30 32-36

Measuring length

1. Cut a piece of string to this length:

2. Use **blue** to colour the objects below that are **longer** than the string.

3. Use **red** to colour the objects below that are **shorter** than the string.

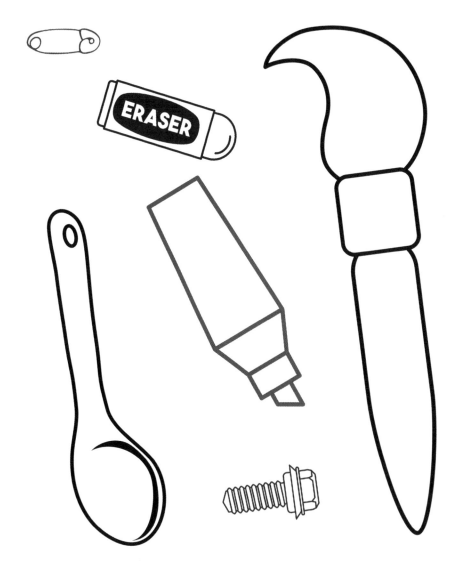

4. What is one thing in your house that is longer than the string?

_____

5. What is one thing in your house that is shorter than the string?

_____

TARGETING HOMEWORK 1 © PASCAL PRESS ISBN 9781925726435

2D shapes

⑥ ▢ Colour the squares blue.

⑦ ⬤ Colour the circles green.

⑧ ▭ Colour the rectangles yellow.

⑨ ◣ Colour the triangles red.

Score 2 points for each correct answer!

SCORE /18 0-6 8-14 16-18

Problem Solving

AC9M1M01, AC9M1SP01

Measuring with your shoe

① Trace around the outside of your shoe. Cut it out.

② Find five things in your house that are **longer** than your shoe and five things that are **shorter** than your shoe. Write them in the box.

Longer than my shoe	Shorter than my shoe

Grammar & Punctuation

AC9E1LA10, AC9E1LA06

Parts of a sentence

Read this sentence:

The baby pig rolled in the mud.

The baby pig tells **who or what** the sentence is about.

rolled tells what is **happening** — what the baby pig did.

in the mud tells more **information** — where the baby pig rolled.

Other sentences might have more information about when, how, why, who or what.

TERM 1 ENGLISH

Read these sentences. Underline the part that tells who or what the sentence is about. Circle the word that tells what is happening.

① The little boy ran to his father.

② The sun shone in the morning.

③ The strong woman lifted the heavy car.

④ The big dog jumped very high.

⑤ The baby cried because he was hungry.

Now answer these questions.

⑥ **Where** did the little boy run? _____

⑦ **How** did the big dog jump? _____

⑧ **When** did the sun shine? _____

⑨ **Why** did the baby cry? _____

⑩ **What** did the strong woman lift? _____

Is it a sentence?

Read each group of words.
Write Yes if it is a sentence. Write No if it is not a sentence.
Underline the capital letters and full stops in each sentence.

⑪ _____ The hungry girl ate the red apple.

⑫ _____ the busy road

⑬ _____ a funny story

⑭ _____ The kangaroo jumped over the fence.

⑮ _____ The children ran across the park.

Score 2 points for each correct answer!

SCORE **/ 30** (0-12) (14-24) (26-30)

Long vowel sounds

Read these pairs of words. **can cane**   **tap tape**

What do you notice?

The **e on the end** of the word helps the **a** say its name, but the **e** says nothing. It is silent.

Now read these words. **pin   pine**   **rip   ripe**

What do you notice?

The **e on the end** of the word helps the **i** say its name, but the **e** says nothing. It is silent.

The e **on the end turns the vowel in the middle from a** short vowel **to a** long vowel.

Write e on the end of each word. Then read the words.

① cak___   ④ snak___

② gat___   ⑤ rip___

③ fiv___   ⑥ pip___

Circle the words that have a long vowel sound.

⑦ rip   hip   sip   bike   ⑨ nap   tape   hat   tap

⑧ pig   pin   pine   pit   ⑩ cane   can   cat   cap

Trace the words. Start at the star. Follow the arrows.

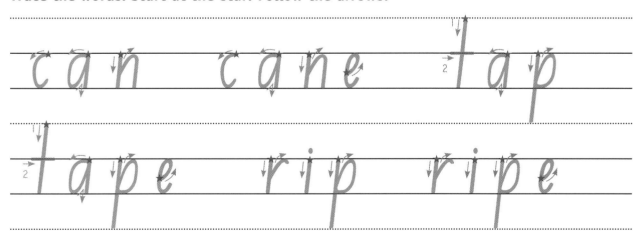

Score 2 points for each correct answer!   SCORE   **/20**   0-8   10-14   16-20

Informative text – Report

TERM 1 ENGLISH

Signs in the City

A city has many signs to help you find your way around.

Some signs tell you what you may and may not do.

Some signs help to keep us safe.

Some signs use words.

Some signs use images.

Some signs use words and images.

Sometimes lights tell us what to do.

Sometimes sounds tell us what to do.

You might see some signs with patterns of bumpy dots. The dots are a special type of writing for people who do not see well. The special writing is called braille. It helps people who are blind find out where they are.

You might also see some coloured patterns of bumpy dots or stripes on the footpaths. These patterns help blind people find their way around the city.

So, words, images, lights and bumps – there are many signs that help us to find our way in the city.

Write or tick the correct answers.

① Why are there lots of signs in the city?

☐ **a** to help us find our way around

☐ **b** to look pretty

☐ **c** to tell us the time

② Look at the signs. Find the sign that looks like this:

Write what it tells you to do.

_____

③ Which sign shows you how to get somewhere?

 a   b   c

④ Which signs tell you it's safe to cross the street?

 a   b   c

⑤ How does a blind person know it is safe to cross the street?

☐ **a** Listen for traffic.

☐ **b** Listen for beeps at the crossing.

☐ **c** Ask someone.

⑥ Which of these signs helps you find your way in the city?

 a   b ☐ c

⑦ Draw a sign that tells you a toy shop is open.

Score 2 points for each correct answer! **SCORE** / 14 (0-4) (6-10) (12-14)

TERM 1 ENGLISH

My Book Review

Title _____

Author _____

Colour stars to show your rating:

Boring   Great!

Comment _____

_____

Number & Algebra

AC9M1N01, AC9M1N04, AC9M1N05

Numbers to 20

1	2	3	4	5	6	7	8	9	10	11	12	13	14	15	16	17	18	19	20

TERM 1 MATHS

Count the objects. Write the number in the box.

① ☐

③ ☐

② ☐

Write the number that comes next.

④ 4, 5, 6, 7, _____

⑤ 2, 4, 6, _____

⑥ 5, 10, 15, _____

Write the missing numbers on these number lines.

⑦

1	2	3			6				10

⑧

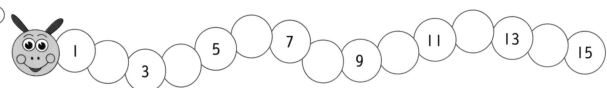

1, 3, 5, 7, 9, 11, 13, 15

⑨ **Look at the 100 grid.**
Some squares are blue.
Write the numbers in these squares in order,
from **smallest** to **largest**.

_____

_____

1	2	3	4	5	6	7	8	9	10
11	12	13	14	15	16	17	18	19	20
21	22	23	24	25	26	27	28	29	30
31	32	33	34	35	36	37	38	39	40
41	42	43	44	45	46	47	48	49	50
51	52	53	54	55	56	57	58	59	60
61	62	63	64	65	66	67	68	69	70
71	72	73	74	75	76	77	78	79	80
81	82	83	84	85	86	87	88	89	90
91	92	93	94	95	96	97	98	99	100

TARGETING HOMEWORK 1 © PASCAL PRESS ISBN 9781925726435

Draw the number of objects in the box.

⑩
9 triangles

⑪
19 circles

Count the sheep in the paddocks. Write how many altogether.

⑫

☐ and ☐ makes ☐

⑭

☐ and ☐ makes ☐

⑬

☐ and ☐ makes ☐

⑮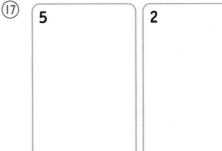

☐ and ☐ makes ☐

Draw the number of flowers in the boxes. Write how many altogether.

⑯
3   4

| 3 | and | 4 | makes | ☐ |

⑰
5   2

| 5 | and | 2 | makes | ☐ |

TERM 1 MATHS

UNIT 4

Score 2 points for each correct answer!

SCORE /34   0-14   16-28   30-34

Time

① Circle the thing that takes the **longest** time.
Draw a star beside the thing that takes the **shortest** time.

A tree grows.

Brush your teeth.

Blow out candles.

② Circle the thing that takes the **longest** time.
Draw a star beside the thing that takes the **shortest** time.

Eat an icecream.

Build a house.

Sleep all night.

Circle the thing that has to **happen first** for each pair of pictures.

③

④

TARGETING HOMEWORK 1 © PASCAL PRESS ISBN 9781925726435

Left and right

Draw a blue circle around the left hand.
Draw a red circle around the right hand red.

⑤ ⑥  ⑦  ⑧  ⑨  ⑩

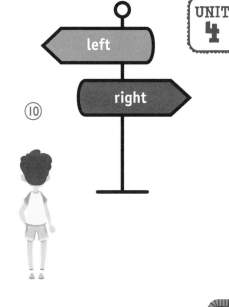

Score 2 points for each correct answer!

SCORE **/20** (0-8) (10-14) (16-20)

Problem Solving

AC9M1SP02

Use the grid to answer the questions.
Tick the correct answers.

① Start at the star. Go up 2 squares,
then go left 2 squares.
What do you find?

 ☐ ☐ ☐

② Start at the star. Go up 2 squares,
then go right 2 squares.
What do you find?

 ☐ ☐  ☐

③ Start at the star. Go down 2 squares,
then go left 2 squares. What do you find?

 ☐ ☐ ☐

④ Start at the star. Go down 2 squares, then go right 2 squares. What do you find?

 ☐ ☐ ☐

⑤ Write how to get from the to the .

_____

_____

17

Parts of a sentence

Read the sentence and then answer the questions.

The farmer milked the cow.

① Who is the sentence about?

_____

② What did the farmer do? _____

③ What did the farmer milk? _____

Read the sentences. Underline the part that tells who or what the sentence is about. Circle the word that tells what happened.

④ The children ate the birthday cake.

⑤ The dog hurt its paw.

⑥ The ball flew over the fence.

⑦ The bird sang loudly.

Read these sentences. Look at the part that is underlined. What does it tell you? Write where, when, how or why.

⑧ The sun rose in the morning. _____

⑨ The frog swam in the pond. _____

⑩ The duck quacked loudly. _____

⑪ The fish stopped to look. _____

The words in these sentences are mixed up. Write them out in order. Look for the capital letters and full stops to help.

⑫ chased kitten the ball. The

_____

⑬ flower. was on A the bee

_____

⑭ after lunch. The played children games

_____

Score 2 points for each correct answer!

SCORE /28 (0-12) (14-22) (24-28)

TARGETING HOMEWORK 1 © PASCAL PRESS ISBN 9781925726435

AC9E1LY09, AC9E1LY11, AC9E1LY08

Long vowel sounds

Read these pairs of words.

 rob robe mop mope not note

What do you notice?

The **e on the end** of the word helps the **o** say its name, but the **e** says nothing. It is silent.

Now read these words.

 cub cube tub tube cut cute

What do you notice?

The **e on the end** of the word helps the **u** say its name, but the **e** says nothing. It is silent.

The e on the end **turns the vowel in the middle from a** short vowel **to a** long vowel.

Write e on the end of each word. Then read the words.

① not____   ③ cub____   ⑤ rop____

② cut____   ④ hop____   ⑥ rul____

Circle the words that have a long vowel sound.

⑦ hop cot dog robe   ⑨ cut cute hum fun

⑧ hot rod rose top   ⑩ rude rug cut mud

Trace the words. Start at the star. Follow the arrows.

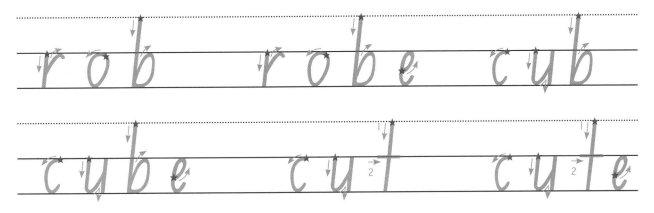

Score 2 points for each correct answer! SCORE **/20**   0-8   10-14   16-20

Reading & Comprehension

AC9EILY01, AC9EILY05

Informative text – Report

Bees

Bees are minibeasts.
They belong to the insect family.
They have three body parts and six legs.
They have four transparent wings.

There are many different kinds of bees.

Some kinds of bees live on their own.
Other kinds of bees live together.
Honeybees live in a hive with other honeybees.

Honeybees fly from flower to flower.
They suck nectar from the flowers.
They pick up pollen on their legs.
They take the nectar and the pollen back to the hive.

Bees make honey from the nectar.
They eat some pollen and some honey.

Bees help people by giving us honey.
They help fruit and vegetables to grow too.

Write or tick the correct answers.

① Which of these statements is true?

　☐ **a** Some bees are insects.

　☐ **b** All bees are insects.

　☐ **c** No bees are insects.

② How many legs do bees have?

　☐ **a** 3

　☐ **b** 4

　☐ **c** 6

③ Bees have transparent wings. What does **transparent** mean?

TARGETING HOMEWORK 1 © PASCAL PRESS ISBN 9781925726435

☐ **a** You can see through them.

☐ **b** You can't see through them.

☐ **c** You can't see them.

④ Where do honeybees live?

☐ **a** on their own

☐ **b** on a flower

☐ **c** in a hive

⑤ Do all bees live in hives?

☐ **a** yes

☐ **b** no

⑥ How do honeybees carry pollen?

☐ **a** on their head

☐ **b** on their legs

☐ **c** in a basket

⑦ What do honeybees eat?

☐ **a** nectar and pollen

☐ **b** nectar and honey

☐ **c** honey and pollen

⑧ What do honeybees use to make honey?

☐ **a** nectar

☐ **b** pollen

☐ **c** nectar and pollen

⑨ Why are bees important?

_____

_____

_____

_____

TERM 1 ENGLISH

Score 2 points for each correct answer!

SCORE **/18** (0-6) (8-14) (16-18)

My Book Review

Title _____

Author _____

Colour stars to show your rating: ☆ ☆ ☆ ☆ ☆

Boring   Great!

Comment _____

_____

Numbers to 20

| 1 | 2 | 3 | 4 | 5 | 6 | 7 | 8 | 9 | 10 | 11 | 12 | 13 | 14 | 15 | 16 | 17 | 18 | 19 | 20 |

Count the objects. Write the number in the box.

① [ ]    ③ [ ]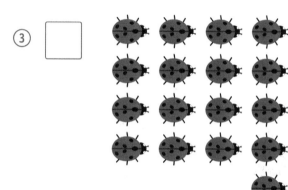

② [ ]

Look the number line at the top of the page. Write the number that comes before.

④ ____ 8   ⑤ ____ 12   ⑥ ____ 17

Write the number that comes after.

⑦ 9 ____   ⑧ 18 ____   ⑨ 13 ____

Write the number that comes between these numbers.

⑩ 12 ____ 14   ⑪ 9 ____ 11   ⑫ 16 ____ 18

Count in 2s. Write the missing numbers.

⑬
| 2 | 4 | 6 | | | 12 | | 16 | | 20 |

⑭

Balloons: 1, 3, 5, [ ], 9, 11, [ ], [ ]

TERM 1 MATHS

(15) How many fingers on these hands? Count by 5s to find how many altogether.

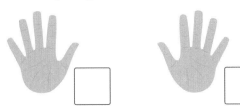  

(16) Look at the 100 grid.
Colour the number squares that help you count in 10s to 100.

(17) Write the numbers you coloured.

_____, _____, _____, _____, _____,

_____, _____, _____, _____, _____

1	2	3	4	5	6	7	8	9	10
11	12	13	14	15	16	17	18	19	20
21	22	23	24	25	26	27	28	29	30
31	32	33	34	35	36	37	38	39	40
41	42	43	44	45	46	47	48	49	50
51	52	53	54	55	56	57	58	59	60
61	62	63	64	65	66	67	68	69	70
71	72	73	74	75	76	77	78	79	80
81	82	83	84	85	86	87	88	89	90
91	92	93	94	95	96	97	98	99	100

Count the birds. Trace the numbers. Write how many altogether.

(18)

$4 + 3 =$

(20)

$2 + 3 =$

(19)

$4 + 2 =$

(21)

$5 + 1 =$

Number & Algebra

Money

22 Tick the coin with the biggest size.   23 Circle the coin with the smallest size.

Look at what you can buy with your coins.

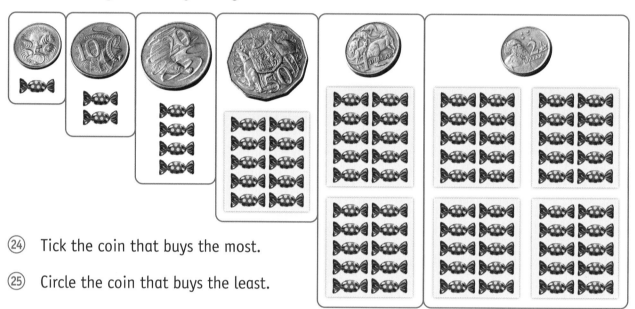

24 Tick the coin that buys the most.

25 Circle the coin that buys the least.

Count the number of coins in each piggy bank.
Circle the coin that buys the most in each piggy bank.

26   27

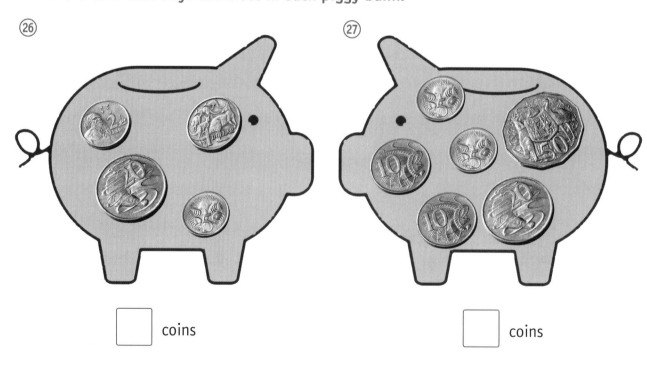

 coins   coins

Score 2 points
for each
correct answer!   SCORE   / 54   0-24   26-48   50-54

TARGETING HOMEWORK 1 © PASCAL PRESS ISBN 9781925726435

TERM 1 MATHS

AC9MIST02

Interpreting a Yes/No graph

Look at the graph. Answer the questions.

Do you have a pet dog?	
🙂	
🙂	
🙂	
🙂	🙂
🙂	🙂
🙂	🙂
Yes	**No**

① How many children have a pet dog? _____

② How many children do not have a pet dog? _____

③ How many children answered the question? _____

④ Which is more? Tick the box.

☐ the number of children who have a pet dog

☐ the number of children who do not have a pet dog

⑤ Do you have a pet dog? Add your answer to the graph.

Score 2 points for each correct answer!

SCORE **/10** (0-2) (4-8) (10)

Problem Solving

AC9MIN01

Sarah has saved some $1 coins in her piggy bank.
Sam wants to know how many there are.

Sarah can't open her piggy bank, so she gave Sam some clues.
Can you work out how many $1 coins Sarah has?

Use the rows of coins to help.
Draw a cross beside the rows that are **not correct**.

Here are Sarah's clues:

• I have more than 4 coins.

• I have fewer than 7 coins.

• I don't have 6 coins.

How many coins does Sarah have? ☐

Grammar & Punctuation

AC9E1LA10, AC9E1LA06

Types of sentences

TERM 1 ENGLISH

A **statement** is a sentence that **gives information**.

  The boy kicked the ball.

A statement begins with a **capital letter** and ends with a **full stop**.

A **question** is a sentence that **asks for information**.

  Who kicked the ball?

A question begins with a **capital letter** and ends with a **question mark**.

Many questions begins with **W words**. Read these questions.

Who did you see at the park?	**What** is your favourite food?
Where did you put the book?	**When** do you play the piano?
Why did the girl go home?	**How** did you make that toy car?

Read this statement.

The girls played football at the park on the weekend.

Finish the questions you could ask about the statement.

① Who _____ ?

② What _____ ?

③ Where _____ ?

④ When _____ ?

Read these sentences. Write S for statement. Write Q for question.

⑤ _____ The sun is bigger than the moon.

⑥ _____ Where did you go yesterday?

⑦ _____ How did the window get broken?

⑧ _____ Why did you do that?

⑨ _____ I saw my friend at the bus stop.

⑩ _____ When did you lose your first tooth?

Score 2 points for each correct answer! **SCORE** **/ 20** (0-8) (10-14) (16-20)

TARGETING HOMEWORK 1 © PASCAL PRESS ISBN 9781925726435

Long a sound when a says its name

Read these words.

 cape cane snake plane cake mate

We can also spell the **long a sound** like this:

 rain chain snail paint hail mail

And like this: **say**   **day**   **may**   **way**   **hay**   **pay**

Choose words from the box above to finish these sentences.

① The _____ flew across the sky.

② The children like to _____ with bright colours.

③ The woman took her dog for a walk every _____.

④ The bag got wet when it was left out in the _____.

⑤ Do you know the _____ to the park?

Long e sound when e says its name

We can spell the **long e sound** like this:

 meat seat seal beach beak bean

We can also spell the **long e sound** like this:

 feet bee sheep wheel queen seed

Choose words from the box above to finish these sentences.

⑥ The bird has a sharp _____.

⑦ The _____ swam deep under the water.

⑧ The man sat down to rest his _____.

⑨ The _____ flew from flower to flower.

⑩ The _____ grew into a huge bean plant.

Score 2 points for each correct answer!

SCORE **/20**   0-8 10-14 16-20

TERM 1 ENGLISH

Trace the words. Start at the star. Follow the arrows.

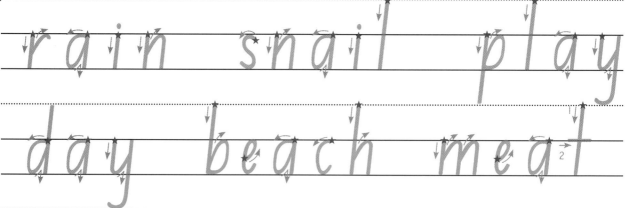

rain snail play

day beach meat

TERM 1 ENGLISH

Reading & Comprehension

AC9E1LY01, AC9E1LY05

Informative text – Procedure

How to Make a Paper-plate Cat Face

For this project you need:
- 1 paper plate for the face
- 2 small paper triangles for ears
- 2 small paper circles for eyes
- 1 very small paper triangle for the nose
- 1 paper crescent for the mouth
- 6 pipe cleaners for whiskers
- glue

What you do:
1 Start with the paper plate.
2 Glue on the two paper triangle ears.
3 Glue on the two paper circle eyes.
4 Glue on the paper triangle nose.
5 Glue on the crescent mouth.
6 Glue on the pipe cleaner whiskers.
7 Give your cat a name!

TARGETING HOMEWORK 1 © PASCAL PRESS ISBN 9781925726435

Reading & Comprehension

Write or tick the correct answers.

① What is the paper plate used for?

☐ **a** eating your dinner

☐ **b** feeding the cat

☐ **c** the cat's face

② How many triangles of paper do you need?

_____

③ What do you know that is shaped like a **crescent**?

_____

_____

④ How many pipe cleaners do you need?

☐ **a** 2   ☐ **b** 4   ☐ **c** 6

⑤ What do you glue onto the plate first?

☐ **a** ears

☐ **b** eyes

☐ **c** mouth

⑥ Why do you need glue?

_____

_____

⑦ What are the pipe cleaners used for?

☐ **a** eyes

☐ **b** ears

☐ **c** whiskers

⑧ If you didn't have a paper plate, what could you use?

☐ **a** a dinner plate

☐ **b** a cardboard circle

☐ **c** nothing

⑨ What is the last thing you glue onto your cat face?

☐ **a** ears

☐ **b** nose

☐ **c** whiskers

⑩ What would you name your cat?

_____

TERM 1 ENGLISH

Score 2 points for each correct answer! **SCORE** **/20** (0-8) (10-14) (16-20)

My Book Review

Title _____

Author _____

Colour stars to show your rating: ☆ ☆ ☆ ☆ ☆

Boring   Great!

Comment _____

_____

Number & Algebra

AC9MIN01, AC9MIN03, AC9MIN04, AC9MIN05, AC9MIN06

Numbers to 20

Use the number grid to count to 20.

1	2	3	4	5	6	7	8	9	10
11	12	13	14	15	16	17	18	19	20

Write the number that comes before.

① _____ 6   ② _____ 19   ③ _____ 11

Write the number that comes after.

④ 14 _____   ⑤ 8 _____   ⑥ 10 _____

Write the number that comes between these numbers.

⑦ 15 _____ 17   ⑧ 11 _____ 13   ⑨ 6 _____ 8

⑩ Look at the number grid. Count the numbers on the orange squares. How are you counting? Circle your answer.

   a by 1s   b in 2s   c in 5s

⑪ On the number grid above, circle the numbers you would use to count in **5s** to 20. Write the numbers on these lines.

   5, _____, _____, _____

⑫ On the number line above, there are 2 rows. How many numbers are in each row? _____

We can also use tallies to count.

1	2	3	4	5	6	7	8	9	10
I	II	III	IIII	ĦĦ	ĦĦ I	ĦĦ II	ĦĦ III	ĦĦ IIII	ĦĦ ĦĦ

Look at these tallies. Write the number. Draw a picture to show how many.

⑬ ĦĦ I _____

⑭ IIII _____

⑮ ĦĦ ĦĦ _____

TARGETING HOMEWORK 1 © PASCAL PRESS ISBN 9781925726435

You need a blue pencil and a yellow pencil.
Colour some shapes blue. Colour the rest yellow. Then add.
The first one is coloured for you.

⑯

_____ + _____ = 7

⑰

_____ + _____ = _____

⑱

_____ + _____ = _____

⑲ Draw a picture to show **3 + 2**. Write the answer.

3 + 2 = _____

TERM 1 MATHS

Sharing

Sam and Sarah have some lollies to share.
They share the lollies so that each child has the same number.

⑳ Draw the lollies that each child has.
Cross off the lollies as you share them.

Sarah's lollies   **Sam's lollies**

   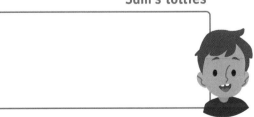

㉑ How many lollies does Sarah have? _____

㉒ How many lollies does Sam have? _____

㉓ The children have _____ lollies each.

Sam and Sarah both want to play with the blocks.
They share the blocks so that each child has the same number.

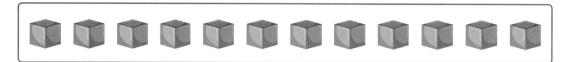

TERM 1 MATHS

(24) Draw the blocks that each child has.
Cross off the blocks as you share them.

Sarah's blocks

Sam's blocks

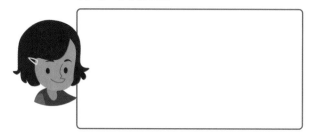

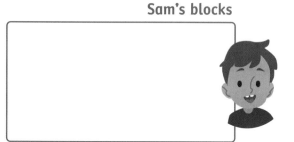

(25) How many blocks does Sam have? _____

(26) How many blocks does Sarah have? _____

(27) The children have _____ blocks each.

Score 2 points
for each
correct answer!

SCORE /52 0-24 26-46 48-52

Measurement & Space

AC9M1M01

Measuring mass

Look at these images.

(1) Cross the objects that are too heavy for you to lift.

(2) Circle the objects that are light enough for you to lift.

③ Look at these images. Circle the object that is heavier than the others.

④ Look at these images. Circle the object that is lighter than the others.

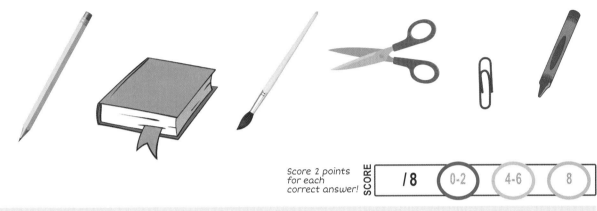

Score 2 points for each correct answer!

SCORE /8 (0-2) (4-6) (8)

AC9M1N05

TERM 1 MATHS

Problem Solving

On the farm there are seven animals:
a dog, a cat, a hen, a goose, a sheep, a horse and a cow.

Sam likes all the animals, but one animal is his favourite.
Can you work out which animal Sam likes best?

Here are the clues:

• It has four legs.

• It is taller than Sam.

• Sam likes to ride it.

Draw a star above Sam's favourite animal.

Grammar & Punctuation

Read the sentences. Underline the part that tells who or what the sentence is about. Circle the word that tells what happened.

① The duck swam in the pond.

② The bee flew from flower to flower.

③ The bird hurt its wing.

④ The children played in the rain.

Read these sentences. Write S for statement. Write Q for question.

⑤ _____ The kangaroo had a baby joey.

⑥ _____ Why did the cat run away?

⑦ _____ Where did you put my book?

⑧ _____ The pencil is on the table.

**Read these sentences. Make sure each sentence begins with a capital letter.
Put a full stop at the end of statements.
Put a question mark at the end of questions.**

⑨ the frog sat on the log

_____

⑩ when are we going home

_____

⑪ why did the dog bark

_____

⑫ my friend is a fast runner

_____

**Look at this picture. Write three questions you could ask about it.
Start with a capital letter and finish with a question mark.**

⑬ _____

_____

⑭ _____

_____

⑮ _____

_____

Score 2 points for each correct answer!

SCORE **/30** 0-12 14-24 26-30

TARGETING HOMEWORK 1 © PASCAL PRESS ISBN 9781925726435

Write the short vowel to complete the word. Use the pictures to help.

① b___g  ③ b___t  ⑤ m___p

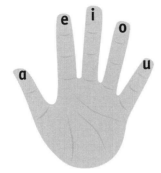

② p___g   ④ f___sh

Circle the word that has a different vowel sound.

⑥ pin bit pine tip

⑦ pot mop rope dog

⑧ cute cut duck sun

⑨ egg hen feet pet

⑩ cap cape cat bag

TERM 1 ENGLISH

These words have **e on the end** to change the **vowel** to the **long sound**:

cake gate time bike note robe cute rule

Choose words from the box above to finish these sentences.

⑪ The girl rode her _____ down the hill.

⑫ The lion cub was very _____.

⑬ I just had _____ to finish my homework.

⑭ I always have chocolate _____ for my birthday.

Each sentence has two words with long vowel sounds. Circle the two words.

⑮ I rode my bike up the hill.

⑯ Our team won the game!

⑰ I will paint a snail for you.

⑱ The sun shines every day.

Trace the words. Start at the star. Follow the arrows.

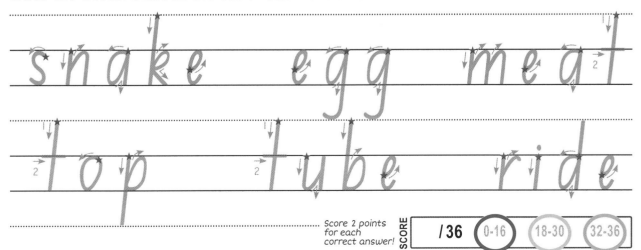

Score 2 points for each correct answer!

SCORE **/36** 0-16 18-30 32-36

| 1 | 2 | 3 | 4 | 5 | 6 | 7 | 8 | 9 | 10 | 11 | 12 | 13 | 14 | 15 | 16 | 17 | 18 | 19 | 20 |

TERM 1 MATHS

Complete this table with numbers, pictures and tallies.

Numbers	Pictures	Tallies
1		
	(2 dots)	||
	(3 dots)	
	(4 dots)	||||
		卌
		卌 |
7	(7 dots)	
8		
		卌 卌
11		卌 卌 |
12		
13	(13 dots)	
		卌 卌 ||||
		卌 卌 卌
	(16 dots)	
	(17 dots)	
		卌 卌 卌 |||
19		
20		

TARGETING HOMEWORK 1 © PASCAL PRESS ISBN 9781925726435

Write the numbers to show how many.

㉑

_____ + _____ = _____

㉒

_____ + _____ = _____

Draw a picture to match. Write how many altogether.

㉓ 7 + 2 = _____

㉔ 4 + 3 = _____

Score 2 points for each correct answer! SCORE / 48 (0-22) (24-42) (44-48)

Measurement & Space

Cut a piece of string to this length: ▬▬▬▬▬▬▬▬

Tick the objects that are longer than the piece of string.
Cross the objects that are shorter.
Circle the objects that are the same length.

①

②

③

④

⑤

⑥

⑦

Score 2 points for each correct answer! SCORE / 14 (0-4) (6-10) (12-14)

Statements and questions

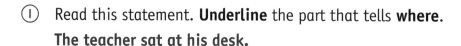

> Question words: Who? Why? What? How? Where? When?

① Read this statement. **Underline** the part that tells **where**.
The teacher sat at his desk.

② Write a question to ask **where**. Remember to use a **question mark**.

Where _____

③ Write a sentence to answer your question.

_____

④ Read this statement. Underline the part that tells **who**.
The girl swam in the river.

⑤ Write a question to ask **who**. Remember to use a question mark.

Who _____

⑥ Write a sentence to answer your question.

_____

Open and closed questions

The questions you wrote are **closed questions**. They have only **one correct answer**.
The answers to closed questions are often yes or no.

Do you have a pet at home? is a closed question. You can only answer **yes** or **no**.

Some questions are **open questions**. They can have many correct answers.
Different people will give different answers:

What is your favourite colour?

How did you get to school?

Why did you do that?

Read these questions. Write O for open (many answers) or C for closed (one answer).

⑦ _____ What is the time?

⑧ _____ What is your favourite food?

⑨ _____ Where do people like to go for holidays?

⑩ _____ Do you like grapes?

Score 2 points for each correct answer!

SCORE **/20** (0-8) (10-14) (16-20)

TERM 2 ENGLISH

Long vowel sounds

An **e on the end** of a word changes the vowel to the **long sound**.
Read these pairs of words. Circle the word with a **long vowel** sound.

① mad made   ② cute cut   ③ robe rob   ④ kit kite

Sometimes we spell the **long a** sound with **ai** or **ay**.
Circle the words with a **long a** sound.

⑤ rain day bat snail paint cap pay

rain   snail   paint

Sometimes we spell the **long e** sound with **ee** or **ea**.
Circle the words with a **long e** sound.

⑥ beet seat set pet sheep bean seal

seat   sheep   seal

Sometimes we spell the **long o** sound with **oa**.
Circle the words with a **long o** sound.

⑦ coat boat cot road rod toad soap

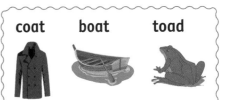
coat   boat   toad

Look at the pictures. Circle the word that is spelt correctly.

⑧ seal sell   ⑨  snail snal   ⑩ got goat

Change the first letter to make new words.

⑪ **goat** ____oat ____oat ____oat ____oat

⑫ **bee** ____ee ____ee ____ee ____ee

⑬ **cake** ____ake ____ake ____ake ____ake

Trace the words. Start at the star. Follow the arrows.

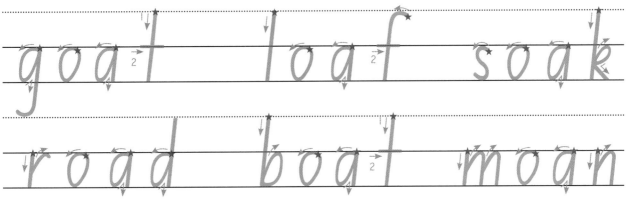

Imaginative text – Poetry

TERM 2 ENGLISH

If You Were an Animal

If you were an animal,

Which would you be?

Would you live on the land,

Or under the sea?

Would you fly through the air,

Or climb in a tree?

Would you run very fast,

Or crawl s-l-u-g-g-i-s-h-l-y?

So many ways to live and explore,
Which would you choose?
(Pause)
Really?

I'd rather be me!

TARGETING HOMEWORK 1 © PASCAL PRESS ISBN 9781925726435

Write or tick the correct answers.

① This piece of writing is

☐ a a letter.

☐ b a poem.

☐ c a story.

② The poem

☐ a asks a question.

☐ b gives a command.

☐ c makes a statement.

③ In the poem, three words rhyme with 'be'. Which word **doesn't** rhyme with 'be'?

☐ a tree

☐ b choose

☐ c me

④ What other word in the poem rhymes with 'be'?

_____

⑤ Complete this question from the poem: **Would you live on the land, or**

_____

⑥ Complete this question from the poem: **Would you fly through the air, or**

_____

⑦ Name one animal that lives on the land.

_____

⑧ Name one animal that runs very fast.

_____

⑨ Which animal would you choose to be? Why?

_____

_____

_____

⑩ What did the poet choose to be?

_____

Score 2 points for each correct answer!

SCORE **/20** (0-8) (10-14) (16-20)

TERM 2 ENGLISH

My Book Review

Title _____

Author _____

Colour stars to show your rating: ☆ ☆ ☆ ☆ ☆

Boring   Great!

Comment _____

_____

Numbers to 30

Look at this number grid.

1	2	3	4	5	6	7	8	9	10
11	12	13	14	15	16	17	18	19	20
21	22	23	24	25	26	27	28	29	30
31	32	33	34	35	36	37	38	39	40
41	42	43	44	45	46	47	48	49	50
51	52	53	54	55	56	57	58	59	60
61	62	63	64	65	66	67	68	69	70
71	72	73	74	75	76	77	78	79	80
81	82	83	84	85	86	87	88	89	90
91	92	93	94	95	96	97	98	99	100

① Start at **2**. Count in **2s** to **30**. Colour the numbers you count.

② Write the numbers here:

2, _____, _____, _____, _____, _____, _____, _____, _____, _____,

_____, _____, _____, _____, 30

③ Start at **20**. Count to **30**. Tick the numbers you count.

④ Write the numbers here:

20, _____, _____, _____, _____, _____, _____, _____, _____, _____, 30

⑤ Count in **5s** to **30**.

5, _____, _____, _____, _____, _____

⑥ On the number grid, circle the numbers that help you count in **10s** to **100**.

⑦ Write the numbers here:

10, _____, _____, _____, _____, _____, _____, _____, _____, 100

⑧ Each of these bags holds 10 marbles. Count in 10s to work out how many marbles altogether. Write the numbers.

10 _____ _____ _____ _____ _____ _____ _____ _____ _____

⑨ Circle the bags you would have if you had 30 marbles.

How many bags did you circle? _____

TERM 2 MATHS

Complete these take away stories.

⑩

5 birds altogether, 2 fly away

_____ birds stay

⑪

6 bees altogether, _____ fly away

_____ bees stay

⑫

_____ dogs altogether, _____ dogs walk away

_____ dogs stay

⑬

_____ coins altogether, _____ crossed out

_____ coins left

Score 2 points for each correct answer!

SCORE **/26** (0-10) (12-20) (22-26)

TERM 2 MATHS

Measurement & Space

AC9M1M01, AC9M1M02, AC9M1SP01

3D Shapes

① Colour the cubes blue.

② Colour the cylinders yellow.

③ Colour the rectangular prisms purple.

④ Colour the spheres red.

⑤ Colour the cones green.

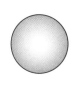     

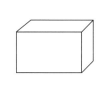

Look at these objects.
Write the name of the 3D shape: cube, sphere, cylinder, cone or rectangular prism.

⑥ _____

⑨ _____

⑦ _____

⑩ _____

⑧ _____

TERM 2 MATHS

Look around your house and find something shaped like these 3D shapes.

⑪ cube _____

⑭ sphere _____

⑫ cylinder _____

⑮ cone _____

⑬ rectangular prism _____

Capacity

Look at these containers for holding water.

(16) Circle the item that will hold the **most** water.

(17) Cross the item that will hold the **least** water.

Get a drinking cup like this:

(18) Find 2 things that hold more than the drinking cup.

_____

_____

(19) Find 2 things that hold less than the drinking cup.

_____

_____

Score 2 points for each correct answer!

SCORE

/38   (0-16)   (18-32)   (34-38)

Problem Solving

AC9M1M02

How many cups does it take to fill a saucepan?

• You use water in this activity, and it might be messy. Ask Mum or Dad where you can do it.

• You need a drinking cup and a saucepan.

• Fill the drinking cup. Make sure the cup is full.

• Pour the water into the saucepan.

• Check to see if the saucepan is full.

• Keep filling the cup and pouring it into the saucepan until the saucepan is full.

• Count how many cups of water you need to fill the saucepan.

How many did you need? ☐

Grammar & Punctuation

AC9E1LA10, AC9E1LA06

TERM 2 ENGLISH

Questions and requests

> **Questions** ask for information. They may be **closed** or **open**.
>
> **Closed questions** have only one correct answer. **Open questions** can have many answers.

Read these questions. Write C for closed (one answer) or O for open (many answers).

① _____ Did you go home after school?

② _____ What is your favourite sport?

③ _____ How many children are in your class?

④ _____ Did you break the window?

> A **request** is another type of question. A request does not ask for information.
> It asks for something, or for someone to do something.
> Requests often use the word **please**.
>
> **Will you close the door please?   Can I have an icecream please?**
>
> **Can I go to Mark's house to play?**

Read these questions. Write C for closed, O for open or R for request.

⑤ _____ What is the capital of Australia?

⑥ _____ Do you like spaghetti?

⑦ _____ Will you make me a sandwich please?

⑧ _____ What do you want to be when you grow up?

⑨ _____ Will you read me a story?

⑩ _____ What is your favourite toy?

Exclamation marks!

> We use a **full stop** at the end of a **statement**.
> We use a **question mark** at the end of a **question**.
>
> We use an **exclamation mark (!)** to show something is exciting or loud, like this:
>
> **Surprise!   Happy birthday!   Bang!   Watch out!   Stop!**

Read these sentences. Put a full stop, question mark or exclamation mark at the end.

⑪ Why did you do that___

⑫ It's a goal___

⑬ Who did you play with at school___

⑭ I saw you at the shops___

⑮ I took my dog to the beach___

Score 2 points for each correct answer!

SCORE /30   (0-12)   (14-24)   (26-30)

TARGETING HOMEWORK 1 © PASCAL PRESS ISBN 9781925726435

AC9E1LY09, AC9E1LY11, AC9E1LY08

Consonant digraphs

sh   When you see the letters **s** and **h** together, they make the **sh sound**, like this:

 shop   **ship**   **sheep**   **shoe**

Write sh at the beginning of these words. Read the words.

① _____ine   ② _____ow   ③ _____ell   ④ _____ed

Read these words.

 fish   **trash**   **dish**   **brush**

Write sh at the end of these words. Read the words.

⑤ bu_____   ⑥ wi_____   ⑦ pu_____   ⑧ ca_____

Underline the sh in these words. Read the words.

⑨ wish   ⑩ shot   ⑪ bush   ⑫ shirt

ch   When you see the letters **c** and **h** together, they make the **ch sound**, like this:

 chain   **chips**   **chick**   **cheese**

Write ch at the beginning of these words. Read the words.

⑬ _____in   ⑭ _____op   ⑮ _____eer   ⑯ _____art

Read these words.

 lunch   **beach**   **couch**   **arch**

Write ch at the end of these words. Read the words.

⑰ ri_____   ⑱ mun_____   ⑲ tea_____   ⑳ mar_____

Underline the ch in these words. Read the words.

㉑ couch   ㉒ chick   ㉓ child   ㉔ bunch

Score 2 points for each correct answer!

SCORE   **/48**   0-22   24-42   44-48

TARGETING HOMEWORK 1 © PASCAL PRESS ISBN 9781925726435

UNIT 11

Trace the words. Start at the star. Follow the arrows.

ship   wash   show

chip   rich   beach

Reading & Comprehension

AC9E1LY01, AC9E1LY05

Informative text – Letter

Dear Grandma

Dear Grandma,

How are you? I miss you. I hope you are feeling better now. Mum said we can come to visit you in the holidays. I can't wait to see you.

At school, we are learning about insects. Last week, I saw three butterflies in our garden. They like the red flowers best. The bees like them too. A man came to school to tell us all about bees. He is a beekeeper. He had some honey for us to taste. It was very sweet.

On Saturday, we played a soccer match. Our team won 4–3. I scored three goals. I got a medal for player of the match. You can see my medal in the photo.

Tonight, we are going to Aunty Marg's for dinner. I am looking forward to playing with Sam and Sarah.

Mum and Dad send their love.

Love from,

Ash xx

TARGETING HOMEWORK 1 © PASCAL PRESS ISBN 9781925726435

Write or tick the correct answers.

① Who is the letter written to?

☐ **a** the child's grandmother

☐ **b** Ash

☐ **c** Mum

② When will Ash visit Grandma next?

☐ **a** tonight

☐ **b** on the weekend

☐ **c** in the holidays

③ How does Ash feel about visiting Grandma?

☐ **a** excited　　☐ **b** sad　　☐ **c** proud

④ What is Ash learning about in school?

☐ **a** soccer

☐ **b** insects

☐ **c** beekeeping

⑤ What did Ash see in the garden?

☐ **a** butterflies

☐ **b** soccer balls

☐ **c** a beekeeper

⑥ What did the beekeeper bring to Ash's school?

_____

⑦ When did Ash play soccer?

☐ **a** at school

☐ **b** on Saturday

☐ **c** in the holidays

⑧ Why did Ash get a medal at soccer?

_____

⑨ Who are Sam and Sarah?

☐ **a** Ash's brother and sister

☐ **b** Ash's aunt and uncle

☐ **c** Ash's cousins

⑩ Why is Ash looking forward to visiting Aunty Marg?

_____

_____

TERM 2 ENGLISH

Score 2 points for each correct answer!　SCORE　**/20**　(0-8)　(10-14)　(16-20)

My Book Review

Title _____

Author _____

Colour stars to show your rating:　☆　☆　☆　☆　☆

Boring　　　　　　　　　　Great!

Comment _____

_____

Number & Algebra

AC9MIN01, AC9MIN03, AC9MIN04, AC9MIN05, AC9MIA01

Numbers to 40

① Look at this number grid. Some of the numbers have fallen off.
Write in the missing numbers.

1	2								10
				16			19		
		23							
	32			35					40

What number comes before?

② _____ 15   ③ _____ 30   ④ _____ 21

What number comes after?

⑤ 39 _____   ⑥ 27 _____   ⑦ 10 _____

What number comes between?

⑧ 23 _____ 25   ⑨ 36 _____ 38   ⑩ 12 _____ 14

⑪ Draw tallies to show 40. The first group of 5 is done for you.

卌 _____ _____ _____ _____ _____ _____ _____

⑫ Write the numbers you use to count in 10s to 40.

_____, _____, _____, _____

How many dots?

⑬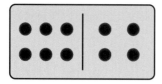

_____ + _____ = _____

⑮

_____ + _____ = _____

⑭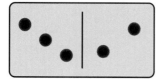

_____ + _____ = _____

⑯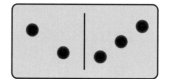

_____ + _____ = _____

TARGETING HOMEWORK 1 © PASCAL PRESS ISBN 9781925726435

Read the take away story. Draw crosses on the picture to show what happens. Write numbers to tell how many are left. Like this:

7 balls, 2 roll away.
5 left

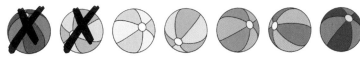

(17) 6 balloons, 2 burst.

_____ left

(18) 9 cookies, 3 are eaten.

_____ left

(19) 5 birds, I flies away.

_____ left

(20) 6 dogs, 3 walk away

_____ left

Score 2 points for each correct answer!

SCORE **/40** (0-18) (20-34) (36-40)

Measurement & Space

AC9M1M03

Time – hour

Look at these clocks. The **big hand** is pointing straight up to the **12**. It is **o'clock**.
The **little hand** tells **what o'clock** it is.

3 o'clock   7 o'clock   10 o'clock   12 o'clock

We can also tell o'clock times like this.

TERM 2 MATHS

What time do these clocks say?

①

_____ o'clock

③

_____ o'clock

⑤

_____

②

1:00

_____ o'clock

④

9:00

_____ o'clock

⑥

4:00

_____

Draw the little hand to show the time on these clocks.

⑦ 3 o'clock

⑧ 6 o'clock

⑨ 11 o'clock

Clockwise

Look at this clock. The hands move around the clock in the direction of the arrows.

The hands go past the numbers in order, from 1, 2, 3, 4 right up to 12. This direction is called **clockwise**.

Wherever you start, clockwise always goes in the same direction as the clock's hands.

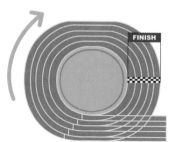

TARGETING HOMEWORK 1 © PASCAL PRESS ISBN 9781925726435

Draw an arrow to show clockwise. Start at the dot.

⑩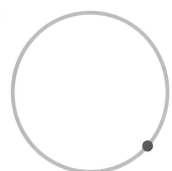

⑪

⑫

Score 2 points for each correct answer! SCORE **/24** (0-10) (12-18) (20-24)

AC9M1N04

Problem Solving

Can you work out which animal was hiding in Sam's garden?

Add the numbers in each box. Draw pictures or tallies to help.

Write the letter in the box above the answer. The letters will spell out the animal.

6   9   5   10   7   8

Z $3 + 2 =$ _____	**A** $5 + 5 =$ _____	**I** $5 + 4 =$ _____
R $6 + 1 =$	**L** $3 + 3 =$ _____	**D** $4 + 4 =$ _____

Requests and commands

TERM 2 ENGLISH

A **request** is a type of question. It asks for something, or for someone to do something. Requests often use the word **please**. The answer might be yes or no.

Will you open the window please?

Can I play outside please?

Can I watch television now?

A **command** tells you what to do. Unlike a request, you may not say yes or no. You must do it. Some commands end with a **full stop**. Some end with an **exclamation mark**.

Read these commands. Compare them to the requests above.

Open the window.

Close your books.

Turn off the television now!

Read these sentences. Write R for request or C for command.

① _____ Will you help your brother, please?

② _____ Come over here!

③ _____ Help your brother.

④ _____ Will you hold the door open, please?

⑤ _____ Go outside and wipe your feet now.

The words in these sentences are mixed up. Write them out in order.
Look for the capital letters, full stops and question marks to help.

⑥ me? Will you with play

_____

⑦ in the children The played playground.

_____

⑧ Go and the door. stand by

_____

⑨ this jar Can you please? open

_____

Score 2 points for each correct answer!

SCORE **/18** (0-6) (8-14) (16-18)

Consonant digraphs

th You make the **th sound** when you put your tongue between your teeth and blow air out. You can hear **th** at the beginning of words like these:

 three   **th**under   **th**ink   **th**row

Write th at the beginning of these words. Read the words.

① _____ank   ② _____in   ③ _____ick   ④ _____irteen

You can hear **th** at the end of words like these:

 too**th**   mo**th**   ba**th**   Ear**th**

Write th at the end of these words. Read the words.

⑤ wi_____   ⑥ bo_____   ⑦ slo_____   ⑧ pa_____

Sometimes you make a **th sound** using your voice too.
You can feel your voicebox vibrate when you say **th** in these words:

the   this   these   those

Sometimes the **th sound** is **voiced** in the middle of words.
Write th in the middle of these words. Read the words.

⑨ fea_____er    ⑩ mo_____er   ⑪ wea_____er

Read these pairs of words. Circle the word in which th is voiced.

⑫ moth mother   ⑬ both bother   ⑭ thin then   ⑮ three feather

⑯ **Name these pictures. Circle the pictures where you can hear a th sound.**

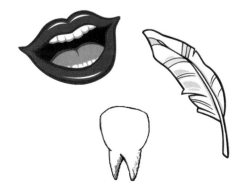         

Score 2 points for each correct answer!

SCORE **/32** 0–24 16–26 28–32

TERM 2 ENGLISH

UNIT 13

Trace the words. Start at the star. Follow the arrows.

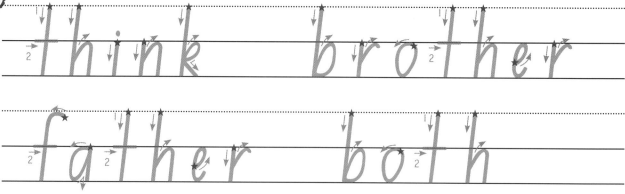

think brother

father both

Reading & Comprehension

AC9E1LY01, AC9E1LY05

Informative text – Diary entries

A Visit to Antarctica

My grandfather went to Antarctica. Every night he sent me an email to tell me what he had seen.

Subject: Day 1

We arrived at Antarctica today. It is very beautiful. I wish you were here with me. I saw six whales. A pod of dolphins swam beside our ship. It was very exciting.

Subject: Day 4

Today we saw hundreds of penguins on the ice. They were very noisy. We saw some seals too.

Subject: Day 2

The sun shines nearly all the time down here. There is always something to see. The icebergs are very white. They look like huge piles of icecream.

Subject: Day 5

We began our trip back home today. We saw more whales and dolphins. It is amazing down here. When you are older, we will come here together.

Subject: Day 3

We went in a glass-bottom boat. We saw hundreds of fish swimming under the boat.

Write or tick the correct answers.

① Who went to Antarctica?

⬚ **a** the child

⬚ **b** the child's family

⬚ **c** the child's grandfather

② How did the grandfather tell the child what he had done?

⬚ **a** He phoned every night.

⬚ **b** He sent an email every night.

⬚ **c** He sent postcards.

③ What swam beside the ship on day 1?

⬚ **a** six whales

⬚ **b** hundreds of fish

⬚ **c** a pod of dolphins

④ What colour are the icebergs?

⬚ **a** white   ⬚ **b** black   ⬚ **c** blue

⑤ What did the grandfather say the icebergs looked like?

_____

⑥ What was special about the boat ride on day 3?

⬚ **a** He saw a lot of sea animals.

⬚ **b** The boat had a glass bottom.

⬚ **c** The boat ran into an iceberg.

⑦ Where were the penguins that the grandfather saw on day 4?

⬚ **a** in the water

⬚ **b** on the ice

⬚ **c** on the iceberg

⑧ How many days did the grandfather have in Antarctica?

_____

⑨ Choose one word that tells you what the grandfather thinks of Antarctica.

_____

⑩ What did the grandfather say he would do one day?

⬚ **a** Never go back to Antarctica.

⬚ **b** Go back to Antarctica.

⬚ **c** Take the child to Antarctica.

Score 2 points for each correct answer!

SCORE **/20** (0-8) (10-14) (16-20)

My Book Review

Title _____

Author _____

Colour stars to show your rating: ☆ ☆ ☆ ☆ ☆

Boring   Great!

Comment _____

_____

Number & Algebra

AC9MIN01, AC9MIN02, AC9MIN04, AC9MIN05

Numbers to 50

Look at these tens frames. Each frame holds ten buttons when it is full.

① Use the buttons on the tens frames to help you count in 10s to 50.

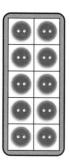 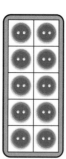 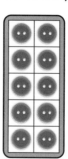 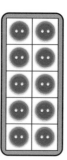 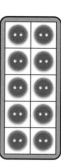

_____   _____   _____   _____   _____

② How many tens frames are there? _____

③ How many buttons are there altogether? _____

Look at these tens frames. They are not full. Count how many buttons on each frame. Write the number on the line.

④ _____   ⑤ _____   ⑥ _____

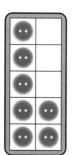   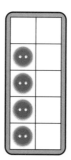   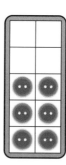

Look at these tens frames. They are not full. How many more buttons do you need to fill the tens frames? Draw the buttons. Write the number.

⑦   ⑧   ⑨

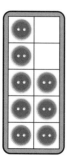   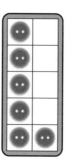   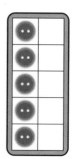

8 + _____ = 10   6 + _____ = 10   5 + _____ = 10

TARGETING HOMEWORK 1 © PASCAL PRESS ISBN 9781925726435

⑩ Look at this number line. Write in the missing numbers.

1	2	3	4			7		10
			14					20

We can show the teen numbers using tens frames. Look at these tens frames. Write how many.

⑪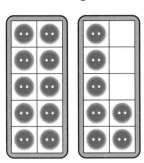

⑫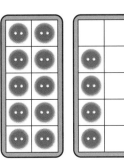

⑬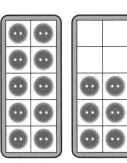

10 and **7** more is _____   **10** and **4** more is _____   **10** and **6** more is _____

Read the take away story. Draw crosses on the picture to show what happens. Write numbers to tell how many are left.

⑭ 7 lollipops. 3 are eaten.

7 take away 3 leaves 4

7 – 3 = ____

⑮ 6 ladybugs. 3 fly away.

6 take away 3 leaves _____

6 – 3 = _____

⑯ 8 fish. 4 swim away.

8 take away 4 leaves _____

8 – 4 = _____

⑰ 5 cars. 3 drive away.

5 take away 3 leaves _____

5 – 3 = _____

⑱ **Make up your own take away stary. Draw a picture to match.**

_____

_____

_____

Number & Algebra

Money

⑲ Circle the biggest coin.

⑳ Cross the smallest coin.

㉑ Tick the coin that can buy the most.

㉒ Colour the coin that is not round.

㉓ Write the values of the coins in order, from least value to most value.

Look at these piggy banks. Count how many dollar coins are in each piggy bank.

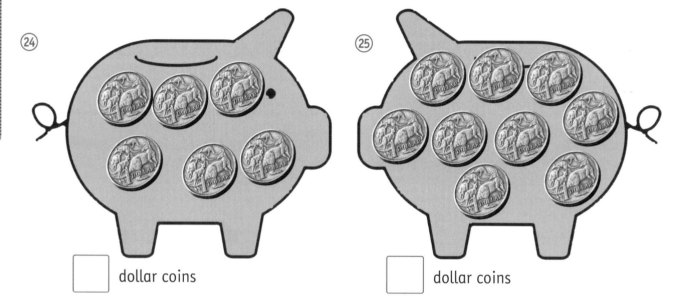

㉔

| | dollar coins

㉕

| | dollar coins

㉖ Circle the piggy bank that has more.

Score 2 points for each correct answer!

SCORE **/52**   0-24   26-46   48-52

Statistics

AC9M1ST02

Using a Graph

Wednesday is Walk to School Day.
The children made this graph.

Did you walk to school today?														
Yes	☺	☺	☺	☺	☺	☺	☺	☺	☺	☺	☺	☺	☺	☺
No	☺	☺	☺	☺	☺	☺	☺	☺	☺					

TARGETING HOMEWORK 1 © PASCAL PRESS ISBN 9781925726435

The children wrote questions to ask about the graph.

Tick the questions that can be answered by the graph.
Cross the questions than cannot be answered by the graph.
Answer the questions you ticked.

① ☐ How many children walked to school?　　_____

② ☐ How many children did not walk to school?　_____

③ ☐ How many children rode bikes to school?　_____

④ ☐ How many children were at school?　　_____

⑤ ☐ How many children were not at school?　_____

⑥ ☐ How many more 'Yes' answers than 'No'?　_____

⑦ If children did not walk, how else could they get to school?

_____

Score 2 points
for each
correct answer!
SCORE
/14　

Problem Solving

AC9M1SP01

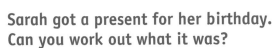

**Sarah got a present for her birthday.
Can you work out what it was?**

Here are the clues.

- Sarah could ride it.

- It has wheels.

- It has handlebars.

- It has no seat.

Draw a circle around Sarah's birthday present.

Grammar & Punctuation

AC9E1LA07, AC9E1LA10

Nouns and pronouns

Nouns are the **names** of people, places and things.
Sometimes we use **pronouns** in place of nouns,
so that we don't have to repeat the nouns.

Read these sentences. The **pronouns** are red.

Tia and Max went to the park. They looked for the playground. It was full of children!

↖They means Tia and Max.   ↖It means the playground.

Read these sentences. The pronouns are underlined. Write what each pronoun means.

① The girl has a ball. <u>It</u> is round. (It means _____.)

② The girl has a ball. <u>She</u> likes to kick the ball. (She means _____.)

③ The children went to the park. <u>They</u> played on the swings.

(They means _____.)

Read this story. Circle the pronouns. There are 11 pronouns.

④ Tia and Max went to the park. They took a ball with them.
It was Tia's ball. She got it at the shops on Saturday.
First, Tia kicked the ball to Max. Then Max kicked it back
to Tia. He kicked it too far. Tia had to run after it.
Then she kicked the ball back to Max. The children played
all afternoon. Then they went home.

Choose pronouns from the box to complete these sentences.

⑤ Look at me. _____ can run fast.

⑥ We have some money. Mum gave it to _____.

⑦ When the girl went to the shops, _____ rode her bike.

⑧ My friends are over there. Can you see _____?

Pronouns
I   me
we   us
you
he   him
she   her
they   them
it

Read these sentences. Circle the pronouns.
Add the missing full stop, questions mark or exclamation mark.

⑨ Did you go to the beach on the weekend_____

⑩ Stop it, right now_____

⑪ I like playing football at the park_____

Score 2 points for each correct answer! **SCORE** **/22** (0-8) (10-16) (18-22)

TARGETING HOMEWORK 1 © PASCAL PRESS ISBN 9781925726435

Consonant digraphs

ph When we see the letters **ph** together, they make a sound like the **letter f** in **feather**. **ph** can be at the beginning, in the middle or at the end of a word.

 phone   photo    elephant   trophy   dolphin

 microphone   gopher   alphabet    graph

Choose words from the box above to complete these sentences.

① A _____ is an animal that lives in the sea.

② The boy took a _____ of his grandfather.

③ Dad played a game on his _____.

④ Lia got a _____ when she won the race.

⑤ Leo danced and sang into the _____.

qu The **letter q** is always followed by the **letter u**. Together they make a sound like **kw**. **qu** can be at the beginning or in the middle of a word.

 queen   quilt   quiet    question   quack

 equals   squid   squirrel   square

Choose words from the box above to complete these sentences.

⑥ A _____ is an animal that lives in the sea.

⑦ The girl answered the _____ in the quiz.

⑧ The duck said _____.

⑨ Two plus two _____ four.

⑩ The _____ wore a gold crown.

Score 2 points for each correct answer!

SCORE **/20** 0-8 10-14 16-20

TERM 2 ENGLISH

Trace the words. Start at the star. Follow the arrows.

elephant phone

square queen squirt

AC9E1LY01, AC9E1LY05

TERM 2 ENGLISH

Reading & Comprehension

Persuasive text – Exposition

Children Need Pets

I want a pet. I want a pet dog more than anything, but my parents say, "No."

Mum says that pets are too messy. Dad says we don't have time to look after a dog. And they cost too much money.

Last time I asked Dad, he said, "No. Not now. Not ever. Never."

But I know I can change his mind. Do you think this will convince him?

Why Children Need Pets

1. When children have a pet to play with, they don't have time to pester their parents.

2. When children take dogs for a walk, they are getting exercise, and exercise is good for us.

3. Children sleep better if they have a pet to sleep with them.

4. Children who have pets are happy.

5. Children who have pets love their parents very much.

P.S. I will feed it and take it for walks and look after it. You won't have to do anything. Please. *Please.*

Reading & Comprehension

Write or tick the correct answers.

① What does the child want?

☐ a a pet

☐ b a pet dog

☐ c a new mum and dad

② Would the child be happy with a pet cat?

☐ a yes   ☐ b no

③ Why doesn't Mum want a dog?

☐ a Dogs are too noisy.

☐ b Dogs cost too much.

☐ c Dogs make too much mess.

④ Which of these did Dad **not** say?

☐ a Dogs have to be walked.

☐ b Dogs take a lot of time.

☐ c Dogs cost a lot of money.

⑤ Who does the child write the list for?

☐ a a friend

☐ b the pet shop owner

☐ c Mum and Dad

⑥ The family already has a pet dog. True or false?

☐ a true   ☐ b false

⑦ How does taking a dog for a walk help the owner?

_____

_____

⑧ What does the child say happens when a pet sleeps with children?

☐ a The children get eaten.

☐ b The children sleep better.

☐ c The children don't go to sleep.

⑨ Which of these does the child **not** promise to do?

☐ a Take the dog for walks.

☐ b Clean up after the dog.

☐ c Wash the dishes.

⑩ Which number in the list do you think is most persuasive? _____

Score 2 points for each correct answer!

SCORE **/20**   (0-8)   (10-14)   (16-20)

TERM 2 ENGLISH

My Book Review

Title _____

Author _____

Colour stars to show your rating: ☆ ☆ ☆ ☆ ☆

Boring   Great!

Comment _____

_____

Number & Algebra

AC9M1N01, AC9M1N03, AC9M1N04, AC9M1N05, AC9M1N06, AC9M1A01, AC9M1A02

Numbers to 60

TERM 2 MATHS

Look at these tens frames. Each frame holds ten buttons when it is full.

① Use the buttons on the tens frames to help you count in 10s to 60.

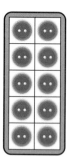 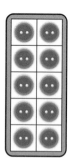 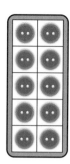 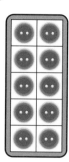 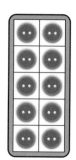 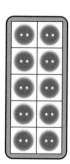

_____   _____   _____   _____   _____   _____

② How many tens frames are there? _____

③ How many buttons are there altogether? _____

④ Use the tallies to help you count in 5s to 60.

卌 卌 卌 卌 卌 卌 卌 卌 卌 卌 卌 卌

_____ _____ _____ _____ _____ _____ _____ _____ _____ _____ _____ _____

Look at the tallies. Write the numbers. Draw hearts to show how many.

	Tallies	Number	Draw hearts
⑤	卌 卌 IIII		
⑥	卌 卌 卌 II		
⑦	卌 卌 III		

Read these number words. Write the number. Draw tallies to match.

	Number word	Number	Tallies
⑧	fourteen		
⑨	sixteen		
⑩	eighteen		

TARGETING HOMEWORK 1 © PASCAL PRESS ISBN 9781925726435

Look at this tens frame.

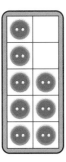

⑪ How many buttons are on the frame? _____

⑫ How many more buttons do you need to make 10? _____

You write the **add story** like this: **7 + 3 = 10**
You can also write the **take away story**.

⑬ The frame should have 10 buttons.
How many buttons are on the frame? _____

⑭ How many buttons are missing? _____

The take away story is: **10 – 7 = 3**

Write an add story and a take away story for these tens frames.

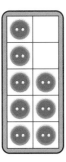

⑮ _____ + _____ = 10

⑯ 10 – _____ = _____

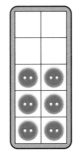

⑲ _____ + _____ = 10

⑳ 10 – _____ = _____

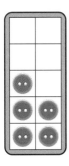

⑰ _____ + _____ = 10

⑱ 10 – _____ = _____

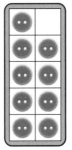

㉑ _____ + _____ = 10

㉒ 10 – _____ = _____

TERM 2 MATHS

Making equal groups

Sam and Sarah made some cookies to sell at the fete.
They decided to put three cookies in each bag.

㉓ Circle groups of three cookies.

㉔ How many bags will Sam and Sarah need? _____

Jake put ten blue socks in the wash. They were all the same.
When they were dry, he put them together in pairs.

㉕ Circle pairs of socks.

㉖ How many pairs of socks does Jake have? _____

Li was hanging balloons for her party.
She wanted to make bunches with five balloons in each.

㉗ Circle groups of five balloons.

㉘ How many bunches of balloons can Li make? ____

There were eight books on the shelf for the prize winners.
Each prize winner received two books.

㉙ Circle groups of 2 books.

㉚ How many prize winners were there? ____

Repeating Patterns

What comes next? Circle the part of the pattern that repeats. Continue the patterns.

㉛  ____ ____

㉜  ____ ____

㉝  ____ ____

㉞ **1 2 3 1 2 3 1 2** ____ ____

Score 2 points for each correct answer!

SCORE | **/ 68** | (0-30) (32-62) (64-68)

TARGETING HOMEWORK 1 © PASCAL PRESS ISBN 9781925726435

TERM 2 MATHS

Sam has 5 pairs of socks.

One pair was red, one pair was blue,
one pair was green, one pair was pink
and one pair was yellow.

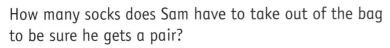

Sam has not put his socks together in pairs.
They are all loose in his sock bag.
Sam takes his socks out his bag one at a time.

How many socks does Sam have to take out of the bag
to be sure he gets a pair?

Write what you think first:

I think he will need to take _____ socks out of the bag.

Now try it. You need 10 small squares of paper (to stand for the socks)
and a bag you can't see through.

Write:

- R for red on two squares
- B for blue on 2 squares
- G for green on 2 squares
- P for pink on 2 squares
- Y for yellow on 2 squares.

Put them into the bag.

Take the squares from the bag one at a time.
Write the colour on the chart: R, B, G, P or Y.
Stop when you have 2 pieces the same colour.

① What number did you stop at? _____

② Try it again. What number did you stop at?

_____

③ Try it again. What number did you stop at?

_____

④ Was it the same number each time? Why?

	Try 1 colour	Try 2 colour	Try 3 colour
1			
2			
3			
4			
5			
6			
7			
8			
9			
10			

TERM 2 MATHS

Grammar & Punctuation

Read these sentences. Write S for statement, Q for question, R for request and C for command.

① _____ Why did you do that?

② _____ Will you close the door please?

③ _____ Who did you see at the shops?

④ _____ Give the book to your brother.

⑤ _____ The boy played in the park.

⑥ _____ The girl rode her bike to school.

⑦ _____ Stop it right now!

⑧ _____ Can I have an apple please?

Read these questions. Write O for open question. Write C for closed question.

⑨ _____ What is your favourite colour?

⑩ _____ How far away is the sun?

⑪ _____ What is your favourite pizza?

⑫ _____ What is the capital of Australia?

⑬ _____ Do you like pizza?

⑭ _____ What colours can flowers be?

Rewrite these sentences correctly. Make each sentence begin with a capital letter and end with a full stop (.) a question mark (?) or an exclamation mark (!).

⑮ where did you put my scooter

_____

⑯ stop that

_____

⑰ i forgot to bring my lunch

_____

Read this story. Write in the pronouns. Choose from the box.

Sam and Sara went to the beach. They played in the water.

Then _____ ⑱ made a sandcastle in the sand.

My brothers and _____ ⑲ went to the beach too. _____ ⑳

didn't see Sam and Sara. They didn't see _____ ㉑ either.

We told _____ ㉒ about our day at the beach

when _____ ㉓ got home.

Pronouns
I   me
we   us
you
he   him
she   her
they   them
it

Score 2 points for each correct answer!

SCORE **/46** (0-20) (22-40) (42-46)

Phonic Knowledge & Spelling

| tail | coat | feet | meat | day | cane | ride | tune | rope | cube |

Choose words from the box above to complete these sentences.

① The toddler put his shoes on the wrong _____.

② The dice is in the shape of a _____.

③ Grandma uses a _____ to help her walk.

④ The horse flicked its _____ as it started to trot.

⑤ The boy put on his _____ before he went outside.

⑥ It is fun to _____ a bike at the park.

⑦ Lions like to eat _____.

⑧ The sun was shining. It was a beautiful _____.

⑨ The boy played a happy _____ on his flute.

⑩ The girl likes to play jump _____ with her friends.

Choose a word from the pair to complete each sentence.

⑪ The _____ sailed all the way across the ocean. (**ship chip**)

⑫ I help my dad _____ vegetables when he cooks. (**shop chop**)

⑬ The genie granted a _____ to the man with the lamp. (**wish witch**)

⑭ We always _____ our hands before dinner. (**wash watch**)

⑮ The young puppy liked to _____ bones. (**shoe chew**)

Read the words. Circle the word that has a different th sound.

⑯ this that thing   ⑱ thirteen those them   ⑳ they think the

⑰ father brother both   ⑲ moth mother feather

Draw lines to match the words to the pictures. Write the beginning sound.

㉑ ____estion

㉒ ____one

㉓ ____oto

㉔ ____ack

Score 2 points for each correct answer!   SCORE   /48   0-22   24-42   44-48

TARGETING HOMEWORK 1 © PASCAL PRESS ISBN 9781925726435

71

Number & Algebra

① Look at this number grid. Write in the missing numbers.

1	2	3	4	⑤	6	7		9	10 ✗
11	12	13	14		16	17	18		20
21		23	24	25	26	27	28	29	
31	32	33	34	35		37	38	39	40
	42	43	44	45	46		48	49	50
51	52			55	56	57	58	59	60

② Colour the numbers to count in 2s. The first one is done for you.

③ Circle the numbers to count in 5s. The first one is done for you.

④ Cross the numbers to count in 10s. The first one is done for you.

⑤ What do you notice about 10, 20, 30, 40, 50 and 60? Circle one answer.

a They are all coloured to count in 2s.

b They are all circled to count in 5s.

c They are all crossed to count in 10s.

d They are all coloured, circled and crossed.

Write the missing numbers in these patterns. Use the number grid to help.

⑥ 16, 18, 20, 22, _____, _____, 28, 30, _____, _____. I am counting in _____.

⑦ 35, 36, 37, _____, _____, 40, 41, _____, _____. I am counting in _____.

⑧ 10, 20, 30, _____, _____, 60. I am counting in _____.

⑨ 5, 10, 15, _____, _____, 30, 35, 40, _____, _____, 55. I am counting in _____.

What number comes before?

⑩ _____ 27   ⑪ _____ 45   ⑫ _____ 58

What number comes after?

⑬ 35 _____   ⑭ 40 _____   ⑮ 23 _____

What number comes between?

⑯ 17, _____, 19   ⑰ 32, _____, 34   ⑱ 40, _____, 42

TARGETING HOMEWORK 1 © PASCAL PRESS ISBN 9781925726435

Count the tallies. Write the number in the box.

⑲ ☐ 卌 卌 ||||

⑳ ☐ 卌 卌 卌 |||

㉑ ☐ 卌 卌 |

㉒ ☐ 卌 卌 ||

㉓ ☐ 卌 卌 卌

㉔ ☐ 卌 卌 卌 ||||

Look at these dominoes. Some of the dots have been hidden.
The total tells how many altogether. Can you work out how many have been hidden?

㉕

3 + _____ = 6

㉖

5 + _____ = 6

㉗

_____ + _____ = 7

㉘

_____ + _____ = 9

Score 2 points for each correct answer! SCORE /56 (0-26) (28-50) (52-56)

Measurement & Space

3D shapes

Draw lines to match the shapes.

①   ②  ③   ④   ⑤

Score 2 points for each correct answer! SCORE /10 (0-2) (4-8) (10)

Grammar & Punctuation

AC9EILA07, AC9EILA10

Nouns and noun groups

TERM 3 ENGLISH

Nouns are the **names** of people, places and things.

A **noun group** is a group of words that tell more about a noun.

These words are **nouns**.

 child   city   car   cow

These are **noun groups**.

a small child   **the busy city**   **this red car**   **her brown cow**

Use each noun to write a noun group.

① cat _____

② cake _____

③ bear _____

④ game _____

Underline the noun groups in these sentences. There are two noun groups in each one. Hint: Look for the nouns first.

⑤ The boy rode his new bike.

⑥ The green frog hopped into the water.

⑦ The children got onto the yellow bus.

⑧ The football team scored three goals.

Proper nouns

Some **nouns** are **proper nouns**. They are the names of specific people, places and things. A proper noun begins with a **capital letter**.

The noun **city** does not need a capital letter, but the **proper noun Canberra** does.

Nouns: country, child   **Proper nouns:** Australia, Ari

Circle the proper nouns in these sentences.

⑨ The teacher asked Ari to open the door.

⑩ The storm caused a blackout in Sydney.

⑪ Stef and I played a game called Angry Goose.

⑫ Kakadu is a famous national park.

Score 2 points for each correct answer!

SCORE **/24** (0-10) (12-18) (20-24)

TARGETING HOMEWORK 1 © PASCAL PRESS ISBN 9781925726435

Consonant digraphs

wh We use these **wh** words for asking questions: **Wh**at? **Wh**y? **Wh**ere? **Wh**en?
When you see the letters **wh** together, they make the **w** sound. The **h** is silent.

Here are some other words with the wh sound. Underline the **wh** in each word.

① wheel   ②  whale   ③ whistle

Write wh at the beginning of these words. Read the words.

④ ____isper   ⑤ ____ite   ⑥ ____eat   ⑦ ____ile

ck When you see the letters **ck** together, they spell the **k** sound.
You will not see **ck** together at the beginning of a word.

Here are some words with the ck sound. Underline the **ck** in each word.

⑧ block   ⑨  duck   ⑩ kick

Write ck at the end of these words. Read the words.

⑪ bla____   ⑫ Ja____   ⑬ ro____   ⑭ li____

ng When you see the letters **ng** together at the end of a word, they spell one sound.
You can hear it in the word **bang**!

Here are some words with the ng sound. Underline the **ng** in each word.

⑮ ring   ⑯ sing   ⑰ spring

Trace the words. Start at the star. Follow the arrows.

thing pick sock

what whisker

Score 2 points for each correct answer!

SCORE /34 (0-14) (16-28) (30-34)

Imaginative text – Narrative

A School for the Animals?

The animal mothers were talking about their children, as all mothers do.

"My boy can climb high," said Mother Monkey. "He can climb higher than anyone."

"I wish my child could," said the other mothers.

"My girl can run fast," said Mother Cheetah. "She can run faster than anyone."

"My girl is strong," said Mother Elephant. "She is stronger than anyone."

"My boy can fly," said Mother Bird. "He can fly further than anyone."

Every time, the other mothers said, "I wish my child could."

"Let's make a school," said the mothers. "Our children can learn everything in school."

They asked Owl to teach their children, but Owl said, "No."

"Your children don't need to be good at everything," she said. "They just need to be best at being themselves."

Write or tick the correct answers.

① What were the mother animals doing?

☐ **a** playing with their children

☐ **b** talking about their children

☐ **c** watching their children

② Which animal was best at climbing?

☐ **a** elephant   ☐ **b** bird   ☐ **c** monkey

TARGETING HOMEWORK 1 © PASCAL PRESS ISBN 9781925726435

3 What was the cheetah best at?

☐ a climbing

☐ b running

☐ c flying

4 Which animal was the strongest?

_____

5 When Mother Bird said her boy could fly further than anyone, she felt

☐ a proud.

☐ b happy.

☐ c disappointed.

6 When Mother Bird said her boy could fly further than anyone, the other mothers felt

☐ a proud.

☐ b happy.

☐ c disappointed.

7 Why did the animal mothers decide to make a school?

☐ a So their children could learn to climb.

☐ b So their children could learn to do everything.

☐ c So their children could learn to swim.

8 Why do you think the mothers asked Owl to teach their children?

_____

_____

9 Do you think Owl could teach all the animals to fly?

☐ a yes   ☐ b no

10 What did Owl **not** tell the mothers?

☐ a You have to be the best at everything.

☐ b You don't have to be good at everything.

☐ c You just have to be the best **you** that you can be.

TERM 3 ENGLISH

Score 2 points for each correct answer!

SCORE **/20** (0-8) (10-14) (16-20)

My Book Review

Title _____

Author _____

Colour stars to show your rating: ☆ ☆ ☆ ☆ ☆

Boring   Great!

Comment _____

_____

Numbers to 80

Look at the 100 grid.

1	2	3	4	⑤	6	7	8	9	10
11	12	13	14	15	16	17	18	19	20
21	22	23	24	25	26	27	28	29	30
31	32	33	34	35	36	37	38	39	40
41	42	43	44	45	46	47	48	49	50
51	52	53	54	55	56	57	58	59	60
61	62	63	64	65	66	67	68	69	70
71	72	73	74	75	76	77	78	79	80
81	82	83	84	85	86	87	88	89	90
91	92	93	94	95	96	97	98	99	100

① Use blue to colour the numbers for counting in 10s to 100. The first one is done for you.

② Write the numbers here.

_____, _____, _____, _____, _____,

_____, _____, _____, _____, _____

③ Circle the numbers you use to count in 5s to 100. The first one is done for you.

④ Use green to colour all the numbers that have a 7 in them.

⑤ What do you notice about the squares you coloured green?

_____

Write the missing numbers in these patterns. Use the 100 grid to help.

⑥ 54, 55, 56, 57, _____, _____, 60, _____, _____.

I am counting in _____.

⑦ 22, 24, 26, _____, 30, _____, 34, _____.

I am counting in _____.

⑧ 25, 30, 35, _____, _____, 50, 55, _____, 65.

I am counting in _____.

⑨ 10, 20, 30, _____, _____, 60, 70, _____.

I am counting in _____.

What number comes after?

⑩ 64 _____   ⑪ 43 _____   ⑫ 27 _____   ⑬ 75 _____

What number comes before?

⑭ _____ 72   ⑮ _____ 66   ⑯ _____ 27   ⑰ _____ 18

TERM 3 MATHS

What number comes between?

⑱ 28 _____ 30   ⑲ 46 _____ 48   ⑳ 71 _____ 73   ㉑ 59 _____ 61

Circle the number that is more.

㉒ 27   72   ㉓ 34   43   ㉔ 62   26   ㉕ 75   57

Look at this tens frame.

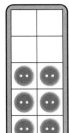

㉖ How many buttons are on the frame? _____

㉗ Draw more buttons to fill the frame. How many buttons did you draw? _____

You can write **2 turnaround addition facts** using this tens frame:
6 + 4 = 10 and 4 + 6 = 10

Look at these tens frames. Draw more buttons to fill each frame.
Write the 2 turnaround addition facts for each frame.

㉘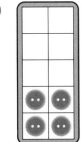

_____ + _____ = _____

_____ + _____ = _____

㉚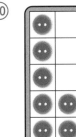

_____ + _____ = _____

_____ + _____ = _____

㉙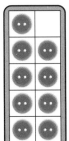

_____ + _____ = _____

_____ + _____ = _____

㉛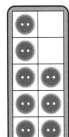

_____ + _____ = _____

_____ + _____ = _____

Draw buttons on these tens frames to show the addition story.
Use two different colours.

㉜ 7 + _____ = 10

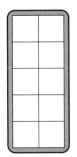

㉝ 5 + _____ = 10

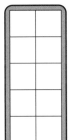

㉞ 8 + _____ = 10

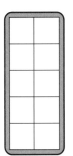

Score 2 points
for each
correct answer!

SCORE / 68   0-32   34-62   64-68

Measurement & Space

AC9MIM01, AC9MIM02, AC9MISP01

Measuring Length

How far to school? Zane, Tara, Jodie and Mark wanted to know who lived closest to school. They looked at the map but they still weren't sure.

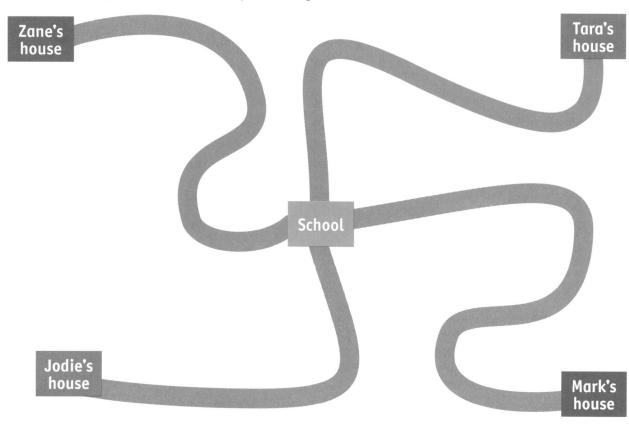

① Predict – who do you think lives closest to school? _____

② Predict – who do you think lives furthest from school? _____

Now measure to see if you are right. You need some five cent coins.

Place the five cent coins along Zane's path, so that the coins are touching each other. Write the number of coins you needed in the box below.
Then measure the paths that Tara, Jodie and Mark take to school.

③ ☐ Zane   ④ ☐ Tara   ⑤ ☐ Jodie   ⑥ ☐ Mark

What did you find out?

⑦ Who lives closest to school? _____

⑧ Who lives furthest away from school? _____

⑨ If you used something else to measure, would you get the same answers? _____

⑩ Use paper clips to measure the paths to check. What did you find out?

_____

TARGETING HOMEWORK 1 © PASCAL PRESS ISBN 9781925726435

2D Shapes

Read the descriptions of these shapes.
Draw lines from the description to the matching shape and name.

⑪
- 4 sides
- 2 long sides
- 2 short sides
- 4 corners

triangle

⑫
- 1 side
- no corners

circle

⑬
- 4 sides
- sides the same size
- 4 corners

rectangle

⑭
- 3 corners
- 3 sides

square

TERM 3 MATHS

Score 2 points for each correct answer!

SCORE

/28   0-12   14-22   24-28

Problem Solving

AC9M1M01

Matt, Jess and Tam measured the cricket pitch.
They put their shoes heel to toe all the way
along the pitch.

Matt counted 111 steps.
Jess counted 105 steps.
Tam counted 100 steps.

① Who took the most steps? _____

② Who has the biggest shoe? _____

③ If you and your father measured the cricket pitch,
who would take the most steps?

_____

④ Do bigger shoes take more or fewer steps?

_____

Plural nouns – adding s

To talk about **more than one** thing, we add **s** to most words.

 one dog three dogs one tree a lot of trees

Draw lines to match the words to the pictures.

①   ③   ⑤

a tin of pencils   one clock   two clocks

a pile of books   a pencil   a book

②   ④   ⑥

Read these sentences. Add s to words that should be more than one.

⑦ The girls rode their bike to school.

⑨ There were seven flower in the bunch.

⑧ I saw three elephant at the zoo.

⑩ All of my pencil are blunt.

The names of the days of the week are proper nouns. They begin with capital letters.

**The letters in these days of the week have been mixed up.
Can you unjumble them?
Make sure each day begins with a capital letter.**

JANUARY						
S	M	T	W	T	F	S
	1	2	3	4	5	6
7	8	9	10	11	12	13
14	15	16	17	18	19	20
21	22	23	24	25	26	27
28	29	30	31			

⑪ ursThday _____

⑫ dayurSat _____

⑬ dayMon _____

⑭ aydFri _____

⑮ Tudayes _____

⑯ unSday _____

⑰ nesWedday _____

Score 2 points for each correct answer!

SCORE **/34** (0-14) (16-28) (30-34)

Consonant blends

bl cl fl gl pl sl

When you see the letter **b**, **c**, **f**, **g**, **p** or **s** followed by the **letter l**, **blend** the two sounds together. You can still hear both sounds.

Listen to the blends at the beginning as you say these words.

black	**cl**oud	**fl**ower	**gl**ass	**pl**ate	**sl**ide

Name these pictures. Write the blend that begins each word.

① _____ 　③ _____ 　⑤ _____ 　⑦ _____

② _____ 　④ _____ 　⑥ _____ 　⑧ _____

Choose one of the words pictured to finish each sentence.

⑨　The sun was shining and the sky was _____.

⑩　The boy picked a _____ for his grandmother.

⑪　The children used _____ to make a town.

⑫　The girl had a _____ of orange juice for breakfast.

⑬　We flew on a _____ to visit our family.

⑭　Everyone had a lot of fun going down the _____.

⑮　The time on the _____ was four thirty.

Trace the words. Start at the star. Follow the arrows.

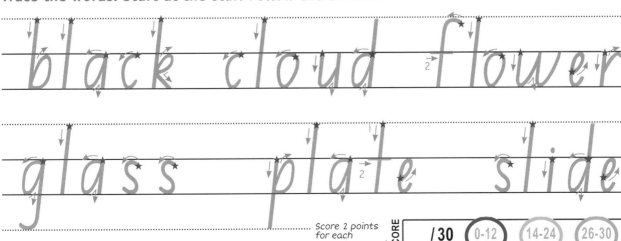

Score 2 points for each correct answer!

SCORE

/30　(0-12)　(14-24)　(26-30)

TERM 3 ENGLISH

Informative text – Report

Alpacas

Alpacas are farm animals. They belong to the same family as camels and llamas.

The first alpacas lived on farms in South America. Now they live on farms in many other places too.

Alpaca hair is used to make clothes and blankets, just like sheep's wool is.

Alpaca hair is softer, silkier and warmer than sheep's wool. It doesn't prickle like sheep's wool sometimes does.

Alpaca hair can be white, black, brown and grey. Sometimes it is dyed to make other colours.

Alpacas live in herds with other alpacas. They are gentle and friendly animals. Sometimes they spit or kick if they are upset or frightened.

Alpacas eat grass and hay. They have short tongues. They have only bottom teeth at the front. They have three stomachs.

Alpacas are quiet animals, but they like to hum.

Write or tick the correct answers.

① What sort of animals are alpacas?

☐ a farm animals

☐ b zoo animals

☐ c wild animals

② Name two other animals in the alpaca family.

_____

③ Where did alpacas first live?

☐ a all over the world

☐ b on farms in South America

☐ c on farms in Australia

TARGETING HOMEWORK 1 © PASCAL PRESS ISBN 9781925726435

④ What is alpaca hair used to make?

☐ **a** sheep's wool

☐ **b** clothes and blankets

☐ **c** books

⑤ Which of these statements is not true?

☐ **a** Alpaca hair is softer than sheep's wool.

☐ **b** Alpaca hair is warmer than sheep's wool.

☐ **c** Alpaca hair prickles like sheep's wool.

⑥ Which of these statements is true?

☐ **a** Alpaca hair can be dyed to make other colours.

☐ **b** Alpaca hair can only be white or brown.

☐ **c** Alpaca babies have purple hair when they are born.

⑦ The name for a group of alpacas is

☐ **a** a pod.

☐ **b** a herd.

☐ **c** a family.

⑧ Write two words that tell about alpacas to finish the sentence.

Alpacas are _____

and _____ animals.

⑨ What do alpacas eat?

☐ **a** wool

☐ **b** other animals

☐ **c** grass and hay

⑩ How many stomachs do alpacas have?

☐ **a** one

☐ **b** two

☐ **c** three

TERM 3 ENGLISH

Score 2 points for each correct answer! SCORE **/20** (0-8) (10-14) (16-20)

My Book Review

Title _____

Author _____

Colour stars to show your rating: ☆ ☆ ☆ ☆ ☆

Boring   **Great!**

Comment _____

_____

Number & Algebra

AC9M1N01, AC9M1N02, AC9M1N03, AC9M1N04, AC9M1N05, AC9M1A01

Numbers to 100

TERM 3 MATHS

Count the number of buttons on these tens frames. Write the number in the box.

① [ ]

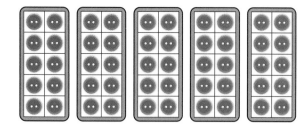

④ [ ]

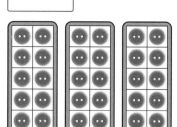

② [ ]

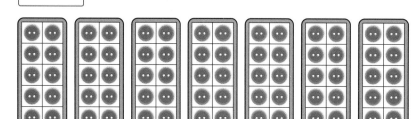

⑤ [ ]

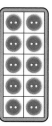

③ [ ]

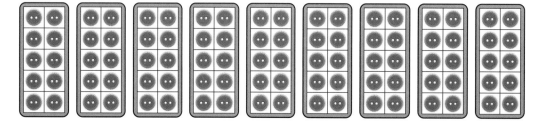

Write the number.

⑥ 5 tens = [ ]   ⑧ 7 tens = [ ]   ⑩ 3 tens = [ ]

⑦ 1 ten = [ ]   ⑨ 8 tens = [ ]   ⑪ 4 tens = [ ]

Complete this table.

⑫ 10 and 7 more		seventeen
⑬ 10 and _____ more		eighteen
⑭ _____ and 4 more	14	
⑮ _____ and _____ more	16	

TARGETING HOMEWORK 1 © PASCAL PRESS ISBN 9781925726435

Write the missing numbers.

(16)

5	10	15	20				45				70

(17)

2	4	6	8					22			

(18)

30	31	32	33				37			41	

(19)

26	25	24	23			20	19	18			

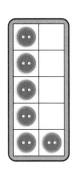

Look at this tens frame. You can write an add story for the frame.

(20) How many buttons are on the frame? _____

(21) How many more buttons do you need to make 10? _____

(22) Write the add story: _____ + _____ = 10

You can also write the **take away story**.

(23) The frame should have 10 buttons. How many are there? _____

(24) How many buttons are missing? _____

(25) Write the take away story: 10 – _____ = _____

Write an add story and a take away story for these tens frames.

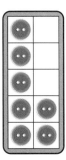

(26) _____ + _____ = 10

(27) 10 – _____ = _____

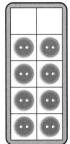

(30) _____ + _____ = 10

(31) 10 – _____ = _____

(28) _____ + _____ = 10

(29) 10 – _____ = _____

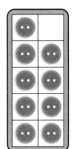

(32) _____ + _____ = 10

(33) 10 – _____ = _____

Score 2 points for each correct answer!

SCORE /66 (0-30) (32-60) (62-66)

TERM 3 MATHS

Measurement & Space

AC9M1M03, AC9M1SP02

Time

August

Sun	Mon	Tues	Wed	Thurs	Fri	Sat
1	2	3	4	5	6	7
8	9	10	11	12	13	14
15	16	17	18	19	20	21
22	23	24	25	26	27	28
29	30	31				

Look at the calendar. Answer these questions.

1. What month is it? _____

2. How many days are there in this month? _____

3. What day of the week is the first day of August? _____

4. What day of the week is the last day of August? _____

5. The weekend days are Saturday and Sunday. Colour all the Saturdays and Sundays.

6. How many Saturdays are there in August? _____

7. How many Sundays are there in August? _____

8. If today is Wednesday, how many days until Saturday? _____

9. If today is Tuesday, what day was yesterday? _____

10. If today is Saturday, what day will tomorrow be? _____

11. Circle the days you go to school.

12. How many school days are there in August? _____

13. How many weekend days are there in August? _____

14. Are there more Tuesdays or more Thursdays in August? _____

TARGETING HOMEWORK 1 © PASCAL PRESS ISBN 9781925726435

Following directions

⑮ Draw the path to show how Red Riding Hood goes to her grandmother's house.

- Start at Red Riding Hood's House.

- Turn left.

- Go past the shop and the church.

- Turn right.

- Go into the park.

- Go around the tree.

- Go between the goal posts.

- Go through the gate.

- Turn right.

- Go over the bridge.

- When you see a sign that says, 'To the woods', turn left.

- Go through the woods. Then you are at Grandma's house.

⑯ Use a different coloured pencil to show another way to Grandma's house.

Score 2 points for each correct answer!

SCORE **/ 32** (0-24) (16-26) (28-32)

Problem Solving

AC9M1M03

Tammie was planning her birthday party.

She wanted to have her party on the weekend.

Some of her friends played sport on Saturday, so that would not do.

① What day would Tammie have her birthday party?

_____

Tammie wanted to have her party in the afternoon.
She wanted it to go for 2 hours.
Her mum said it had to finish at 3 o'clock.

② What time would Tammie's party start? _____

③ Show the start time on this clock.

Grammar & Punctuation

AC9E1LA10, AC9E1LY15

Plural nouns – adding es

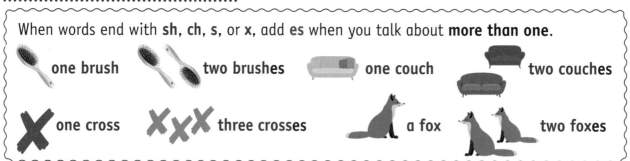

When words end with **sh, ch, s,** or **x,** add **es** when you talk about **more than one**.

one brush   two brushes   one couch   two couches

one cross   three crosses   a fox   two foxes

Draw lines to match the words to the pictures.

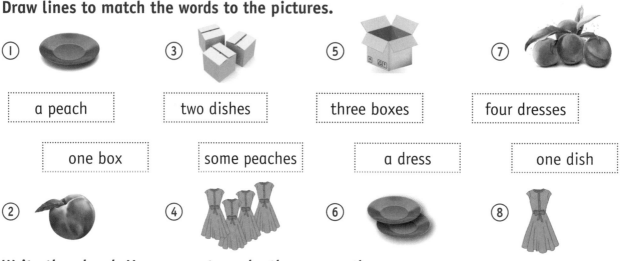

① ③ ⑤ ⑦

a peach   two dishes   three boxes   four dresses

one box   some peaches   a dress   one dish

② ④ ⑥ ⑧

Write the plural. Use s or es to make them more than one.

⑨ spider _____   ⑫ mix _____

⑩ crash _____   ⑬ beach _____

⑪ torch _____   ⑭ bus _____

Proper nouns

The months of the year are proper nouns. They begin with **capital letters**.
Rewrite these sentences correctly. Make sure each month begins with a capital letter.

⑮ My birthday is in june.

_____

⑯ We are going to the circus in october.

_____

⑰ Our summer holidays start in december.

_____

Score 2 points for each correct answer! **SCORE** **/34** (0-14) (16-28) (30-34)

TARGETING HOMEWORK 1 © PASCAL PRESS ISBN 9781925726435

Consonant blends

br cr dr fr gr pr tr

When you see the letter **b**, **c**, **d**, **f**, **g**, **p** or **t** followed by the **letter r**, **blend** the two sounds together. You can still hear both sounds.

Listen to the blends at the beginning as you say these words.

brown   **crab**   **drum**   **frog**   **grass**   **present**   **train**

TERM 3 ENGLISH

Look at the pictures. Write the blend that begins each word: **br**, **cr**, **dr**, **fr**, **gr**, **pr** or **tr**.

① _____   ③ _____   ⑤ _____   ⑦ _____

② _____   ④ _____   ⑥ _____   ⑧ _____

Choose one of the words pictured above to finish each sentence.

⑨ The _____ jumped off the lily pad and into the water.

⑩ The prince gave a _____ to the dragon.

⑪ Our new house is made of brown _____ .

⑫ We walked across the _____ tracks and into the station.

⑬ I like to lie on the _____ and look at the sky.

⑭ One man plays a _____ and the other men dance.

⑮ The _____ scuttled across the sand and down a hole.

Trace the words. Start at the star. Follow the arrows.

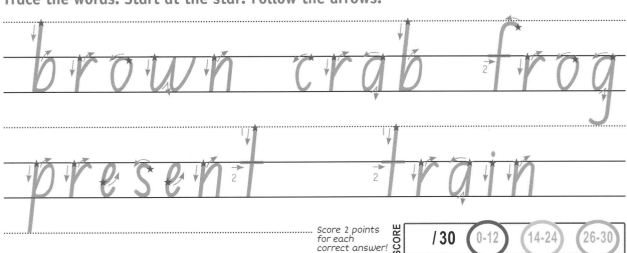

Score 2 points for each correct answer!

SCORE

/30   0-12   14-24   26-30

Informative text – Report

TERM 3 ENGLISH

Recount – Our Field Trip to the Lake

Yesterday, our class went to the lake to look for minibeasts. We took a magnifying glass and a notebook.

The first minibeasts we saw were dragonflies. Two big red dragonflies were flying above the water. Their bodies were very shiny. We could see their four transparent wings.

Next, we saw some bees flying around the flowers. The bees had black and yellow stripes on their bodies. They were collecting pollen from the flowers.

Dragonflies

After that, we saw a big group of beetles. They were blue with red spots. They were running up and down the tree trunk.

We saw a lot of spider webs at the lake. Some webs did not have spiders in them. Some webs had flies and other insects in them. Some spiders were big, and some were small.

Spider webs

We saw a lot of minibeasts at the lake. We were sad when we had to go back to school. We would like to go to the lake again another day.

Write or tick the correct answers.

① When did the class go to the lake?

_____

② Why did the class go to the lake?

_____

TARGETING HOMEWORK 1 © PASCAL PRESS ISBN 9781925726435

③ What did the children take with them to the lake?

☐ a a microscope

☐ b a microphone

☐ c a magnifying glass

④ Why did the children take a notebook to the lake?

☐ a to draw a picture of the lake

☐ b to write about what they saw

☐ c to write a letter to their parents

⑤ How many wings does a dragonfly have?

☐ a two

☐ b four

☐ c six

⑥ What is another word for **transparent**?

☐ a colourful

☐ b shiny

☐ c see-through

⑦ Where did the bees collect pollen?

☐ a from the lake

☐ b from the flowers

☐ c from the dragonflies

⑧ What colour were the beetles?

_____

⑨ How many spiders did the children see at the lake?

☐ a a lot

☐ b 100

☐ c a few

⑩ How did the children feel about their trip to the lake?

☐ a happy

☐ b sad

☐ c disappointed

TERM 3 ENGLISH

Score 2 points for each correct answer! **SCORE** /20 (0-8) (10-14) (16-20)

My Book Review

Title _____

Author _____

Colour stars to show your rating: ☆ ☆ ☆ ☆ ☆

Boring   Great!

Comment _____

_____

Number & Algebra

AC9M1N01, AC9M1N02, AC9M1N03, AC9M1N05, AC9M1A01

Numbers to 100

1	2	3	4	5	6	7	8	9	10
11	12	13	14	15	16	17	18	19	20
21	22	23	24	25	26	27	28	29	30
31	32	33	34	35	36	37	38	39	40
41	42	43	44	45	46	47	48	49	50
51	52	53	54	55	56	57	58	59	60
61	62	63	64	65	66	67	68	69	70
71	72	73	74	75	76	77	78	79	80
81	82	83	84	85	86	87	88	89	90
91	92	93	94	95	96	97	98	99	100

**Look at the 100 grid.
It helps you count up to 100
and back from 100.**

① Colour the numbers that help you count in 10s to 100.

② Circle the numbers that help you count in 5s to 100.

③ Start at 22. Count in 2s to 42. Write the numbers you count.

22, _____, _____, _____, _____, _____,

_____, _____, _____, _____, _____

④ Find the last number you counted and colour it red.

⑤ Start at 64 and count in 1s to 74. Write the numbers you count here.

64, _____, _____, _____, _____, _____, _____, _____, _____, _____, _____

⑥ Find the last number you counted and colour it yellow.

⑦ Use blue to colour all the numbers that have a 9 in them. What do you notice?

_____

⑧ Write the numbers that come between 33 and 40.

33, _____, _____, _____, _____, _____, _____, 40

⑨ Write the numbers that come between 57 and 61:   57, _____, _____, _____, 61

⑩ Write the numbers that come between 78 and 82:   78, _____, _____, _____, 82

Count backwards in 1s. Write in the missing numbers.

⑪ 10, 9, 8, _____, _____, _____, _____, _____, _____, _____

⑫ 19, 18, _____, _____, _____, _____, _____, _____, _____, _____

⑬ 59, 58, 57, _____, _____, _____, _____, _____, _____, _____

⑭ 76, 75, 74, _____, _____, _____, _____, _____, _____, _____

TARGETING HOMEWORK 1 © PASCAL PRESS ISBN 9781925726435

Draw buttons on the frames to show the number.

(15) 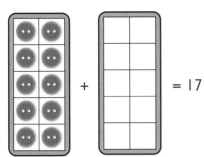 + [   ] = 17

(17) 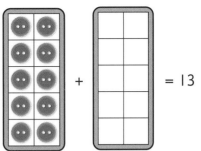 + [   ] = 13

(16) 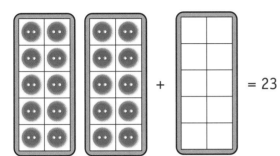 + [   ] = 23

(18) 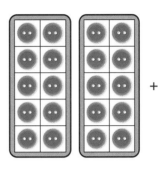 + [   ] = 26

Write the add stories.

(19)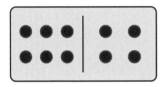

_____ + _____ = _____

(21)

_____ + _____ = _____

(20)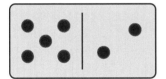

_____ + _____ = _____

(22)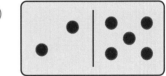

_____ + _____ = _____

Money

There are 100 cents in $1.

(23) Colour the 5 cent coins as you count them in 5s to 100. Stop when you get to 100.

(24) How many coins did you colour? _____

(25) How many 5c coins do you need to make $1? _____

TERM 3 MATHS

㉖ Colour the 10 cent coins as you count them in 10s to 100. Stop when you get to 100.

㉗ How many coins did you colour? _____

㉘ How many 10c coins do you need to make $1? _____

㉙ Colour the 20 cent coins as you count them in 20s to 100. Stop when you get to 100.

㉚ How many coins did you colour? _____

㉛ How many 20c coins do you need to have $1? _____

Score 2 points for each correct answer! **SCORE** | /62 | 0-28 | 30-56 | 58-62

Statistics

AC9M1ST01

Interpreting Data

How many lollies in the lolly jar?

Draw tallies for each of the lollies in the jar. Cross off the lollies as you count them.

① _____

② _____

③ _____

④ _____

TERM 3 MATHS

⑤ Show your information on this graph.

⑥ Draw the lolly that has the most.

⑦ Draw the lolly that has the least.

⑧ How many ✦ are there?

⑨ Which has more, ♥ or ◉ ?

⑩ How many more? _____

8				
7				
6				
5				
4				
3				
2				
1				

Score 2 points for each correct answer!

SCORE **/20** (0-8) (10-14) (16-20)

Problem Solving

AC9M1N01

How many people in Riley's family?

The children played a game to guess how many people in their families.
It was Riley's turn. Can you work out the number of people in Riley's family?

Use the rows of people to help.
Draw a cross beside the rows that are **not correct**.

These are the questions the children asked.

- Are there less than seven?
  Riley said, "Yes."

- Are there more than three?
  Riley said, "Yes."

- Are there more than five?
  Riley said, "No."

- Are there four?
  Riley said, "No."

How many children are in Riley's family?

_____

Grammar & Punctuation

AC9EILA10, AC9EILY15

Plural nouns – irregular

Some words **don't change** when there is **more than one**.

 one **sheep**   three **sheep**   one **fish**   two **fish**

one **deer**, two **deer**   one **shrimp**, two **shrimp**

Some words change to a **new word** when there is **more than one**.

one **child**, two **children**   one **foot**, two **feet**   one **mouse**, three **mice**

Choose a word from the box above to complete these sentences.

① Lucy had different socks on her _____ .

② Chen invited three _____ to play at his house.

③ The farmer had ten woolly _____ in her paddock.

④ The fisherman caught four _____ in his net.

⑤ The cat chased the _____ into its hole.

Choose the correct word from the brackets to complete these sentences.

⑥ Lots of _____ came to watch the show. (person, people)

⑦ The _____ all wore flowers in their hair. (woman, women)

⑧ The dentist made sure all my _____ were clean. (tooth, teeth)

Capital letters

Whenever you write **I** to mean yourself, it needs a capital letter.
The **names of people** begin with capital letters too.

Read these sentences. Circle the words that should begin with a capital letter.

⑨ When jacob came to my house, i showed him my fish.

⑩ The teacher told susie and mia to go outside.

⑪ Mr lee liked the apples that i picked for him.

⑫ Dad said that sam could go with zara and me to the park.

⑬ My friend nico can run faster than me.

Score 2 points for each correct answer!

SCORE /26   (0-10)   (12-20)   (22-26)

TARGETING HOMEWORK 1 © PASCAL PRESS ISBN 9781925726435

TERM 3 ENGLISH

Consonant blends

sc sk sm sn sp st sw

When you see these letter groups, **blend** the two sounds together.
You can still hear both sounds.

Listen to the blends at the beginning as you say these words.

scooter	**sk**ates	**sm**ile	**sn**ake	**sp**ider	**st**op	**sw**ing

Look at these pictures. Write the blend that begins each word.

① _____    ③ _____   ⑤ _____   ⑦ _____

② _____   ④ _____   ⑥ _____   ⑧ _____

TERM 3 ENGLISH

tw When we see these two letters together, sometimes we blend the two sounds.

The **w** is **silent** in the word **two**, 2. We can't hear it.

But we can hear the **w** in these words that are built from **two**.

 twelve   **tw**enty   **tw**ins   **tw**ice

You can also hear the **tw** blend in these words.

 twig   **tw**eet   **tw**eezers   **tw**ine

Choose one of the words pictured on this page to finish each sentence.

⑨ The girl rode her _____ down the hill.

⑩ The bird gathered small _____ to make its nest.

⑪ A long black _____ was hiding in the grass.

⑫ The children sang Twinkle Twinkle Little _____ at the concert.

⑬ The _____ liked to do everything together.

⑭ The children played on the _____ in the park.

Score 2 points for each correct answer!

SCORE **/28** (0-12) (14-22) (24-28)

Trace the words. Start at the star. Follow the arrows.

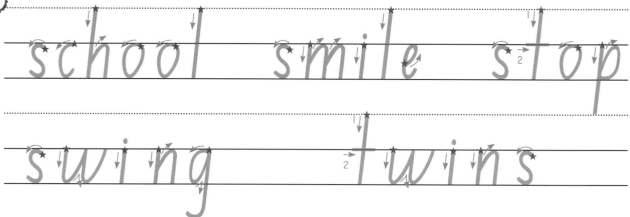

school smile stop

swing twins

Reading & Comprehension

AC9E1LY01, AC9E1LY05

Informative text – Procedure

How to Make a Healthy, Smiley-face Sandwich

Ingredients – things you need:

- 1 slice of wholemeal bread
- 1 slice of cheese
- 1 cherry tomato
- 2 slices of cucumber
- 1 slice of capsicum
- alfalfa sprouts

What you do:

1 Start with the bread.

2 Put on the cheese.

3 Put on the cucumber eyes.

4 Put on the capsicum mouth.

5 Put on the cherry tomato nose.

6 Put on the alfalfa hair.

7 Eat and enjoy!

Write or circle the correct answers.

1. This piece of writing is

   ☐ **a** a poem.

   ☐ **b** a recipe.

   ☐ **c** a story.

2. This piece of writing tells

   ☐ **a** how to make a book.

   ☐ **b** about healthy food.

   ☐ **c** how to make a sandwich.

3. The word **ingredients** means

   ☐ **a** things you need.

   ☐ **b** things you do.

   ☐ **c** things you say.

4. Which of these is another word for **healthy**?

   ☐ **a** unhealthy

   ☐ **b** delicious

   ☐ **c** nutritious

5. Which of these ingredients do you **not** need?

   ☐ **a** butter

   ☐ **b** bread

   ☐ **c** cheese

6. What do you need the cucumber for?

   ☐ **a** the mouth

   ☐ **b** the nose

   ☐ **c** the eyes

7. What do you put on the bread first?

   ☐ **a** the cucumber

   ☐ **b** the cheese

   ☐ **c** the alfalfa

8. What do you put on last?

   _____

9. What is the last thing you do to your sandwich?

   _____

10. Is the sandwich good for you to eat?

   ☐ **a** yes   ☐ **b** no

TERM 3 ENGLISH

Score 2 points for each correct answer!

SCORE **/20** (0-8) (10-14) (16-20)

My Book Review

Title _____

Author _____

Colour stars to show your rating: ☆ ☆ ☆ ☆ ☆

Boring   Great!

Comment _____

_____

Number & Algebra

AC9M1N01, AC9M1N02, AC9M1N04, AC9M1N05, AC9M1N06

Numbers to 100

Look at the 100 grid. It helps us count up to and back from 100.

Colour the number of each answer on the grid.

1	2	3	4	5	6	7	8	9	10
11	12	13	14	15	16	17	18	19	20
21	22	23	24	25	26	27	28	29	30
31	32	33	34	35	36	37	38	39	40
41	42	43	44	45	46	47	48	49	50
51	52	53	54	55	56	57	58	59	60
61	62	63	64	65	66	67	68	69	70
71	72	73	74	75	76	77	78	79	80
81	82	83	84	85	86	87	88	89	90
91	92	93	94	95	96	97	98	99	100

① 41, 42, 43, 44, _____, 46, 47

② 40, 45, 50, 55, 60, _____, 70, 75

③ 48, 50, 52, 54, _____, 58, 60

④ 68, 67, 66, 65, _____, 63, 62

⑤ 35, 40, 45, 50, _____, 60, 65

⑥ The number between 43 and 45 is _____.

⑦ The number that is one more than 53 is _____.

⑧ The number that is one less than 67 is _____.

⑨ The number that comes after 45 is _____.

⑩ The shape you made by colouring the grid is a _____.

⑪ Circle all the numbers on the grid that have a 2 in them. What do you notice?

_____

Write what you know about these numbers.
For example: 12 is 1 row of ten and 2 more

⑫ 22 is ____ rows of ten and 2 more

⑬ 32 is ____ rows of ten and 2 more

⑭ 42 is ____ rows of ten and 2 more

⑮ 52 is ____ rows of ten and 2 more

⑯ 62 is ____ rows of ten and 2 more

⑰ 72 is ____ rows of ten and 2 more

⑱ 82 is ____ rows of ten and 2 more

⑲ 92 is ____ rows of ten and 2 more

Doubles

Write the doubles facts you see on these dice.

⑳

_____ + _____ = _____

㉑

_____ + _____ = _____

TARGETING HOMEWORK 1 © PASCAL PRESS ISBN 9781925726435

㉒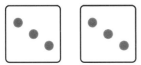

_____ + _____ = _____

㉔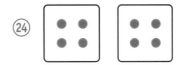

_____ + _____ = _____

㉓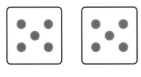

_____ + _____ = _____

㉕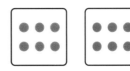

_____ + _____ = _____

Double and **add 1** to complete these number facts.

㉖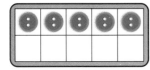

5 + 5 + 1 = _____

㉘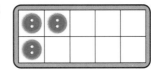

_____ + _____ + 1 = _____

㉗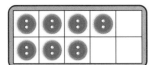

_____ + _____ + 1 = _____

㉙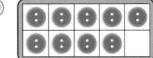

_____ + _____ + 1 = _____

Draw lines to match the number, the picture and the add story.

㉚ 18   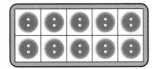    10 + 2

㉛ 15   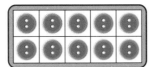   10 + 8

㉜ 12   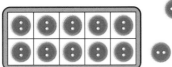    10 + 7

㉝ 17   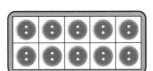   10 + 5

Sharing

Zara and Tema have 8 cars. They share them so that each child has the same number.

TERM 3 MATHS

(34) Draw the cars to show how many each child has. Cross out the cars as you draw them.

Zara's cars

Tema's cars

(35) How many toy cars does Zara have? _____

(36) How many toy cars does Tema have? _____

The children each have half of the cars.

Jaz and Zane have 12 chocolates. They want to share them to have half each.

(37) Draw the chocolates to show how many each child gets. Cross out the chocolates as you draw them.

Jaz's chocolates

Zane's chocolates

(38) How many chocolates do Jaz and Zane each get? _____

Circle half of each group.

(39)

(40)

Measuring mass

Look at these balance scales. Circle the object that is heavier.

①    ②    ③

Look at these objects and balance scales. Draw the missing object on the scales.

④ 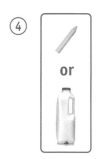    ⑤

Score 2 points for each correct answer!   SCORE   **/10**   (0-2)   (4-8)   (10)

TERM 3 MATHS

Problem Solving

AC9M1SP01

Whose toy?

Jaz, Zara, Zane and Tema all brought a toy to school for the class display.
Can you work out which toy belongs to which child?
Draw lines to match the child and the toy.

Here are the clues:

- Jaz brought a toy with wheels.
- Tema brought a toy that makes him think.

- Zane brought a toy that could roll.
- Zara brought a toy that has long ears.

Jaz   Zara   Zane   Tema

Grammar & Punctuation

Nouns are the names of people, places and things.
A noun group is a group of words that tell more about a noun.

Circle the nouns in these sentences.

① The children rode their new bicycles.

② The hungry boy ate his lunch very quickly.

③ The quiet girl built a city with her blocks.

Underline the noun groups in these sentences.

④ The lonely scarecrow stood in the field.

⑤ The red car went very fast down the long straight road.

Proper nouns are the names of specific people, places and things.
A proper noun begins with a capital letter.

Choose proper nouns from the box to complete these sentences.

| August | Canberra | Miss Vogel | Wednesday |

⑥ I have soccer training every _____.

⑦ We are going on a school trip to Uluru in _____.

⑧ My teacher's name is _____.

⑨ _____ is the capital city of Australia.

Choose the correct word from the brackets to complete these sentences.

⑩ Nala cleaned her _____ every night. (tooth, teeth)

⑪ Alex put all the _____ in the sink. (brush, brushes)

⑫ The teacher gave all of the _____ a sticker. (child, children)

⑬ Song had one more _____ than Finn. (sticker, stickers)

Write the word for more than one (plural).

⑭ crab _____

⑮ fish _____

⑯ sheep _____

⑰ mouse _____

⑱ fox _____

Score 2 points for each correct answer!

SCORE **/36** (0-16) (18-30) (32-36)

TARGETING HOMEWORK 1 © PASCAL PRESS ISBN 9781925726435

Word finder

These words are hidden in the grid below.

black	crown	fruit	present	smile	swing
brown	dragon	glass	scarecrow	snake	tree
cloud	flower	grapes	skeleton	spider	twenty
crab	frog	plate	slide	stop	twinkle

The words go from left to right or top to bottom.
When you find a word, circle the letters and tick the word in the list above.
Can you find all 24 words?

b	l	a	c	k	a	s	c	a	r	e	c	r	o	w
r	z	y	r	q	i	k	j	z	a	k	l	q	w	r
o	t	h	a	r	y	e	e	t	b	n	o	m	y	l
w	w	s	b	j	g	l	p	k	f	r	u	i	t	u
n	e	t	t	r	e	e	f	l	l	p	d	o	w	i
x	n	u	h	g	e	t	s	t	o	p	o	n	i	q
a	t	s	d	f	c	o	d	v	w	b	n	m	n	w
z	y	x	s	w	i	n	g	y	e	t	r	c	k	e
q	u	r	p	v	w	u	i	f	r	o	g	o	l	p
r	s	m	i	l	e	d	h	d	f	j	r	k	e	l
e	n	t	d	s	c	f	j	e	g	h	a	c	v	p
u	a	z	e	c	r	a	s	d	z	x	p	b	n	l
t	k	o	r	v	o	g	p	r	e	s	e	n	t	a
y	e	p	a	b	w	n	g	l	a	s	s	b	m	t
d	r	a	g	o	n	m	k	l	a	s	l	i	d	e

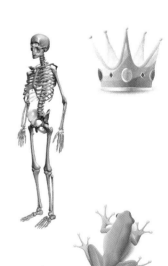

Score 2 points for each correct answer!

SCORE **/48** 0-22 24-42 44-48

Number & Algebra

Write the missing numbers.

①
27	28	29			32	33				37			40

②
72	73	74				78					83		

③
34	36		40	42	44				52	54			60

④
5	10	15	20				45						70

⑤
10	20	30					80		

⑥
66	65	64	63				59				55		

⑦
18	17	16							10				

⑧ **Start at the star. Colour the box in which the numbers add to 10.**
Find the box next to it in which the numbers add to 10. Colour it.
Find and colour the path of boxes in which the numbers add to 10.

Which shape do you finish next to?

5 + 1	8 + 0	3 + 5	7 + 2	2 + 6	3 + 2	5 + 3	4 + 2	7 + 1
■	5 + 3	9 + 1	8 + 2	3 + 7	4 + 6	1 + 9	5 + 1	♥
7 + 0	6 + 1	6 + 4	6 + 3	5 + 2	7 + 1	10 + 0	9 + 0	3 + 6
2 + 1	2 + 7	5 + 5	7 + 3	★	2 + 4	2 + 8	5 + 2	5 + 4
4 + 5	3 + 4	5 + 3	2 + 5	4 + 5	3 + 1	7 + 3	6 + 3	2 + 3
▲	6 + 1	3 + 3	4 + 1	2 + 2	6 + 2	0 + 10	8 + 2	●
6 + 2	4 + 4	6 + 4	5 + 4	0 + 3	2 + 7	5 + 0	6 + 2	4 + 3

How many buttons altogether? Write the number in the box.

⑨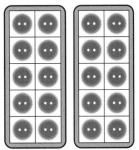

⑫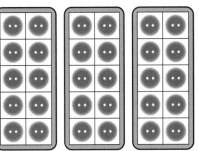

⑩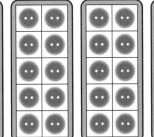

⑬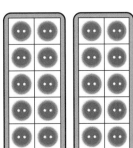

⑪

Count the value of the coins in each purse. Write the total.

⑭ _____

A

⑯ _____

C

⑮ _____

B

⑰ _____

D

⑱ Which box has the most money? _____

⑲ Which box has the least money? _____

Score 2 points for each correct answer!

SCORE | /38 (0-16) (18-32) (34-38)

109

Grammar & Punctuation

AC9EILA06, AC9EILA07

Verbs

> **Verbs** are **action words** that tell you what is **happening.** For example, **swims** and **play.**

Underline the verb in each sentence – the part that tells what is happening.

① The boy ran to school.

② The sun shines brightly.

③ The girl eats her lunch.

④ The dog chased the cat.

Read these words. Write N for noun or V for verb.

⑤ ☐ ball

⑥ ☐ stopped

⑦ ☐ summer

⑧ ☐ ate

⑨ ☐ danced

⑩ ☐ played

⑪ ☐ games

⑫ ☐ grow

⑬ ☐ feet

> Some **verbs** are **being verbs.** They tell you the **state** of something.
>
> For example: **The dog was wet.**
>
> This sentence tells you about the state of the dog – wet. The **being verb** is **was.**
> Some other **being verbs** are **is, am, were** and **are.**

Underline the being verb in each sentence – the part that tells you the state.

⑭ The cat is friendly.

⑮ The children are naughty.

⑯ I am thirsty.

⑰ The sun is bright.

⑱ The game was difficult.

⑲ The people were noisy.

Choose your own action verb or being verb to complete each sentence.

⑳ The girl _____ very fast.

㉑ The door _____ open.

㉒ The car _____ down the road.

㉓ The dogs _____ on the beach.

㉔ The teacher _____ grumpy.

㉕ The tree _____ in the garden.

㉖ The boy _____ the game.

Score 2 points for each correct answer!

SCORE / 52 0-24 26-46 48-52

TARGETING HOMEWORK 1 © PASCAL PRESS ISBN 9781925726435

Vowel sounds

> Some letters can have more than one sound.

For each list, circle the word in which a has a different sound.

① cat hand all apple

③ fast father last late

② wash wait watch want

④ fall walk pal tall

For each list, circle the word in which u has a different sound.

⑤ cute music use but

⑦ blue bug flute glue

⑥ cut put up fun

⑧ put push pull pup

For each list, circle the word in which o has a different sound.

⑨ hot stop rope dog

⑪ home not open no

⑩ love some done pot

⑫ box robe hop odd

For each list, circle the word in which e has a different sound.

⑬ met meet pen bed

⑮ be see sweet wet

⑭ end seed wheel free

⑯ teeth egg pet yes

For each list, circle the word in which i has a different sound.

⑰ bit bite lid rip

⑲ ride file sing bike

⑱ ripe tip pig pin

⑳ like wild five trip

Trace the words. Start at the star. Follow the arrows.

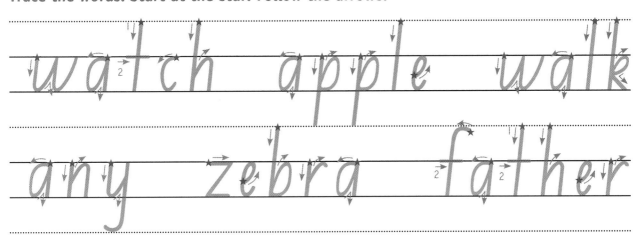

watch apple walk

any zebra father

TERM 4 ENGLISH

Score 2 points for each correct answer!

SCORE /40 0-18 20-34 36-40

Imaginative text – Poetry

A Guinea Pig

Anonymous (circa 1775)

There was a little guinea pig,

Who being little, was not big;

He always walked upon his feet,

And never fasted when he eat.

When from a place he run away,

He never at the place did stay;

And while he run, as I am told,

He never stood still for young or old.

He often squeaked, and sometimes violent,

And when he squeaked he never was silent.

Though never instructed by a cat,

He knew a mouse was not a rat.

One day, as I am certified,

He took a whim, and fairly died;

And as I am told by men of sense,

He never has been living since.

Write or circle the correct answers.

① This piece of writing is

☐ **a** a letter.

☐ **b** a story.

☐ **c** a poem.

② The poem is about

☐ **a** a pet pig.

☐ **b** a guinea pig.

☐ **c** a giant pig.

③ The guinea pig was

☐ **a** little. ☐ **b** big. ☐ **c** giant.

④ The guinea pig liked to sleep a lot. True or false?

☐ **a** true ☐ **b** false

⑤ Which of these did the guinea pig like to do?

☐ **a** Stay very still.

☐ **b** Run away.

☐ **c** Eat cats.

⑥ What noise did the guinea pig make?

_____

⑦ Which of these statements is true?

☐ **a** The guinea pig thought a mouse was a rat.

☐ **b** The guinea pig thought a cat was a rat.

☐ **c** The guinea pig knew a mouse was not a rat.

⑧ In the poem, find a word that rhymes with **pig**.

_____

⑨ In the poem, find a word that rhymes with **old**.

_____

⑩ What happened to the guinea pig at the end of the poem?

☐ **a** It died.

☐ **b** It ran away.

☐ **c** It was eaten by the cat.

TERM 4 ENGLISH

Score 2 points for each correct answer!

SCORE **/20** (0-8) (10-14) (16-20)

My Book Review

Title _____

Author _____

Colour stars to show your rating: ☆ ☆ ☆ ☆ ☆

Boring   Great!

Comment _____

_____

Number & Algebra

AC9M1N01, AC9M1N02, AC9M1N04, AC9M1N05, AC9M1A01

Numbers to 100

TERM 4 MATHS

We can show numbers to 100 using tens frames, like this.

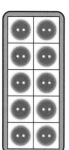 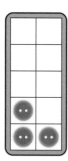

We can write: 1 ten and 3 ones = 13
or 10 + 3 = 13

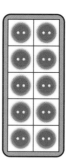 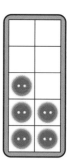

We can write: 2 tens and 5 ones = 25
or 20 + 5 = 25
or 10 + 10 + 5 = 25
or 10 + 15 = 25

Look at these tens frames. Write the number you see in different ways.

①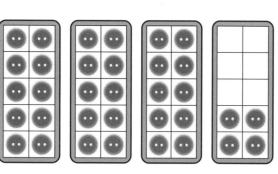

____ tens and ____ ones = ____

or ____ + ____ = ____

or ____ + ____ + ____ + ____ = ____

or ____ + ____ + ____ = ____

②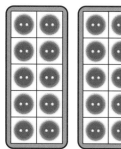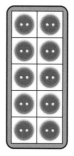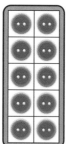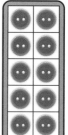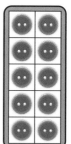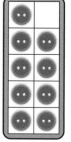

____ tens and ____ ones = ____

or _____

or _____

or _____

or _____

TARGETING HOMEWORK 1 © PASCAL PRESS ISBN 9781925726435

We can also show numbers using tens rods and unit blocks.

■■■■■■■■■■ ■■■■ = 1 ten and 4 ones = 14

Write the number of blocks you see.

③ = _____ tens and _____ ones = _____

④ = _____ tens and _____ ones = _____

Count the number of ones blocks in these tens rods.
Write the total at the end of each line.

⑤ ■■■■■■■■■■ _____

■■■■■■■■■■ _____

■■■■■■■■■■ _____

■■■■■■■■■■ _____

■■■■■■■■■■ _____

■■■■■■■■■■ _____

■■■■■■■■■■ _____

■■■■■■■■■■ _____

■■■■■■■■■■ _____

■■■■■■■■■■ _____

Ten tens = one hundred = 100

Read these number stories. Draw the picture in the box. Write the addition fact.

⑥ Martin had 6 marbles in one hand.
He had 9 marbles altogether.
How many marbles were in his other hand?

6 + _____ = 9

⑦ Claire had 5 red blocks.
She had 10 blocks altogether.
How many blocks were not red?

5 + _____ = 10

⑧ Tema had 10 toy cars.
He had 7 racing cars.
How many cars were not racing cars?

7 + _____ = 10

Score 2 points
for each
correct answer!

SCORE **/16** 0-6 8-12 14-16

TARGETING HOMEWORK 1 © PASCAL PRESS ISBN 9781925726435

3D shapes

Read the descriptions of the shapes.
Draw lines from the description to the matching shape.
Write the name of the shape in the box.
Choose from these names: **cube, sphere, cylinder, cone, rectangular prism.**

①
- 12 edges
- 8 corners
- 6 square faces

②
- no edges
- no corners
- 1 curved face

③
- 1 edge
- 1 corner
- 1 curved face
- 1 circular face

④
- 2 edges
- no corners
- 1 curved face
- 2 circular faces

⑤
- 12 edges
- 8 corners
- 6 faces
  (4 long and 2 short)

Write the name of the 3D shape: **cube, sphere, cylinder, cone** or **rectangular prism.**

⑥   _____

⑦ _____

⑧ _____

⑨   _____

⑩  _____

TARGETING HOMEWORK 1 © PASCAL PRESS ISBN 9781925726435

Capacity - Full and empty

Look at the glasses.

⑪ Draw a circle around the glass that is full.

⑫ Draw a cross on the glass that is empty.

⑬ Tick the glass that is half full.

⑭ Draw a line under the glass that is nearly full.

⑮ Draw a star on the glass that is nearly empty.

TERM 4 MATHS

Score 2 points for each correct answer! SCORE
/30 0-12 14-24 26-30

Problem Solving

AC9M1M01

Can you show on the glasses how much juice each child has?

- Tema has less juice in his glass than Sam has.
- Sasha has more juice than Sam.
- Sam's glass is half full.
- None of the glasses is full and none of the glasses is empty.

Tema's glass	Sasha's glass	Sam's glass

Grammar & Punctuation

AC9E1LA06, AC9E1LA07

Verbs – word families

> You change the **end of a verb** to show **who** is doing the action.
>
> I **walk**. We **walk**. You **walk**. They **walk**.   She **walks** and he **walks** and a dog **walks** too.

Write the correct form of the verb to complete each sentence.

① The man _____ up the hill every day. (walk, walks)

② I _____ my bike to school. (ride, rides)

③ She always _____ her homework. (do, does)

④ They _____ at the beach when it is hot. (swim, swims)

> You change the **end of a verb** or **add an extra word** to show **when** the action happens.
>
> I **play**.   now – the present   She **plays**.
> I **played**.   yesterday – the past   She **played**.
> I **will play**.   tomorrow – the future   She **will play**.

Write the correct form of the verb in brackets to show that the action happens now.

⑤ The boy _____ to school in the rain. (run)

⑥ Dad _____ to the music. (dance)

⑦ The horses _____ over the fence. (jump)

Write the correct form of the verb to show that the action will happen in the future.

⑧ Leo and I _____ for our parents. (wait)

⑨ Hana _____ in the band next year. (play)

> Some verbs change in different ways to show the **past**.
>
> Today I **ride** my bike. Yesterday I **rode** my bike.
> Today we **swim** in the pool. Yesterday we **swam** in the pool.

Write the correct form of the verb in brackets to complete each sentence.

⑩ Yesterday, the wild wind _____ down the big tree. (blows, blew)

⑪ Yesterday, we _____ our books to the library. (take, took)

⑫ Yesterday, I _____ a funny story. (write, wrote)

Score 2 points for each correct answer!   SCORE   /24   0-10   12-18   20-24

Matching sounds

These words all begin with the same **s** sound: **s**ent **c**ent **s**illy **c**ity **s**ome **c**ycle
Circle the word that does **not** begin with the **s sound.**

① sound   circle   sheep   same
② cell   centre   circus   call   same

These words all have the **long i** sound: **ride fly night sign pie buy**
Circle the word that does **not** have the **long i sound.**

③ bike   fight   by   eight   die
④ cry   might   pie   bit   height

These words all have the **long a** sound: **chain plane day eight they steak**
Circle the word that does **not** have the **long a sound.**

⑤ weight   splat   grain   say   skate
⑥ snail   man   pane   say   freight

These words all have the **f** sound: **fish phone after elephant thief graph**
Circle the word that does **not** have the **f sound.**

⑦ dolphin   puppy   found   father
⑧ feather   phantom   fast   grape

These words all have the **long e** sound: **bee sea thief monkey puppy these**
Circle the word that does **not** have the **long e sound.**

⑨ chief   donkey   mummy   eight
⑩ funny   set   meet   these   seat

These words all have the **long o** sound: **goat toe nose window though no**
Circle the word that does **not** have the **long o sound.**

⑪ blow   pool   rose   go   boat
⑫ gone   go   ghost   gopher   goat

Trace the words. Start at the star. Follow the arrows.

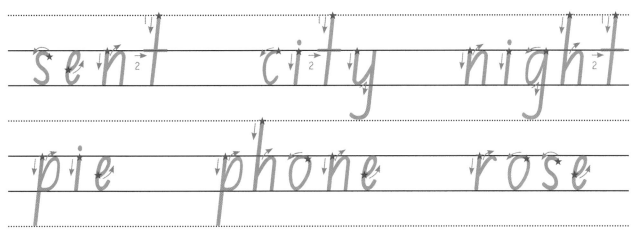

Score 2 points for each correct answer!

SCORE

/24   (0-10)   (12-18)   (20-24)

TERM 4 ENGLISH

Informative text – Report

TERM 4 ENGLISH

An Incident at School

New Message

To: Ash@email.com.au

Subject: Something bad happened at school today

Hi Ash,

Something bad happened at school today. I was playing with my friends. There was a new kid too. He only came to our school last week. He is nice and we let him play with us.

Some big kids came over. They were mean to the new kid for no reason. He didn't do anything. He was just playing with us. The big kids laughed at him and called him names. They said no one wanted to be his friend. He started to cry and ran away.

I went after him. I told him I wanted to be his friend. I asked, "Why were they being so mean to you?"

He said the big boy used to go to his old school. He was mean to him there too. That's why the new kid came to this school. He wanted to get away from the mean kid. But now the mean kid is here too. The new kid begged me not to tell anyone. I'm worried that the big kid will keep being mean.

What do you think I should do?

Your cousin,

Sarah

Write or circle the correct answers.

① Who is the email written to? _____

② Who wrote the email?

☐ **a** Ash

☐ **b** Ash's sister Sarah

☐ **c** Ash's cousin Sarah

(3) Where did the incident happen?

☐ **a** at home

☐ **b** at school

☐ **c** at the park

(4) When did the incident happen?

☐ **a** in class

☐ **b** at lunch

☐ **c** on the weekend

(5) The new kid at school is

☐ **a** mean.

☐ **b** a bully.

☐ **c** nice.

(6) Why did the new kid cry and run away?

☐ **a** He didn't like Sarah and her friends.

☐ **b** Sarah was being mean to him.

☐ **c** Some big kids were being mean to him.

(7) Why did Sarah go after the new kid?

☐ **a** to help him

☐ **b** to be mean to him

☐ **c** to tell him to stay away

(8) How did the new kid feel when he was being bullied?

☐ **a** brave

☐ **b** upset

☐ **c** happy

(9) How does Sarah feel?

☐ **a** worried

☐ **b** happy

☐ **c** proud

(10) What do you think Sarah should do?

_____

_____

Score 2 points for each correct answer! **SCORE** **/ 20** (0-8) (10-14) (16-20)

My Book Review

Title _____

Author _____

Colour stars to show your rating: ☆ ☆ ☆ ☆ ☆

Boring   Great!

Comment _____

_____

Numbers more than 100

We can also show numbers up to 99 using tens rods and ones blocks.

Write the number of blocks you see.

① = _____ tens and _____ ones = _____

② = _____ tens and _____ ones = _____

When we have ten rods, each with 10 ones blocks, we have 100 blocks.

③ Count the number of ones blocks
in these tens rods.

Write the total at the end of each line.

_____

_____

_____

_____

_____

_____

_____

_____

_____

_____

We show 100 with a flat grid.
Look at these blocks. Write the number you see.

④ one hundred and three

= _____ + _____ = _____

⑤ one hundred and six

= _____ + _____ = _____

⑥ **Look at this number line. Write the missing numbers.**

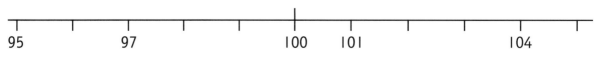

95   97   100 101   104

TARGETING HOMEWORK 1 © PASCAL PRESS ISBN 9781925726435

Read these number stories. Draw the picture in the box. Write the subtraction fact.

⑦ Sue had 6 marbles. Some rolled away.
She has three left.
How many rolled away?

6 – _____ = 3

⑧ Claire had 10 red blocks.
She gave some to Sam. She has 5 left.
How many did she give to Sam?

10 – _____ = 5

⑨ Martin baked 12 cupcakes.
He and his brother ate some.
There are 6 left. How many were eaten?

12 – _____ = 6

⑩ Tema had 9 toy cars.
He gave some to his friend.
He has 4 cars left.
How many cars did he give to his friend?

9 – _____ = 4

TERM 4 MATHS

Score 2 points for each correct answer! **SCORE** **/20** (0-8) (10-14) (16-20)

Measurement & Space

AC9M1M03, AC9M1SP02

Time

When the **big hand** is pointing straight up to the **12**, it is **o'clock**.
The **little hand** tells **what o'clock** it is.

Write the time.

① _____ o'clock

② _____ o'clock

③ _____

When the **big hand** points straight down to **6**, it has gone **halfway** around the clock from 12. It tells you that it is **half past** the hour. The **little hand** has moved past the hour and is halfway to the next number.

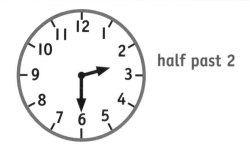

half past 2

TERM 4 MATHS

Write the time.

④ half past _____

⑤ half past _____

⑥ half past _____

Draw the big hand on these clocks to show **half past. Write the time.**

⑦ half past _____

⑧ half past _____

⑨ half past _____

Following Directions

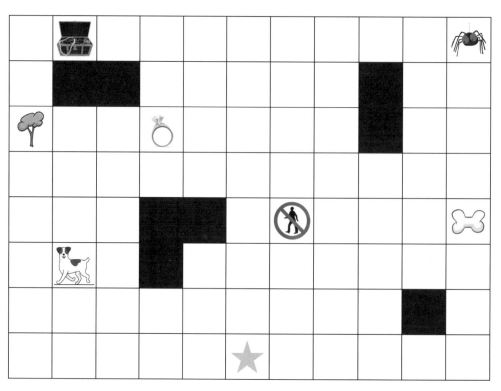

TARGETING HOMEWORK 1 © PASCAL PRESS ISBN 9781925726435

Follow the directions. Draw the paths as you go.
Use a different colour for each path.

(10) Start at the star.

Go right 3.

Go up 4.

Go left 6.

Go up 1.

Go left 2.

Where are you? ☐

(11) Start at the star.

Go left 3.

Go up 4.

Go right 5.

Go down 1.

Go right 3.

Where are you? ☐

(12) Start at the star.

Go up 2.

Go right 2.

Go up 4.

Go left 3.

Go up 1.

Go left 3

Where are you? ☐

Score 2 points for each correct answer!

SCORE /24 ⬤0-10 ⭕12-18 ⭕20-24

TERM 4 MATHS

Problem Solving

AC9M1SP02

Use the grid opposite.

(1) Count the number of squares it took you to get from the star to the treasure.

_____

(2) Colour the squares in the shortest path from the star to the treasure.

How many squares did you colour? _____

(3) Write the directions here.

Start at the star.

_____

_____

_____

Grammar & Punctuation

AC9E1LA06, AC9E1LA07

Adjectives

TERM 4 ENGLISH

> **Adjectives** tell you more information about **nouns**.
>
> They might tell you **what kind** – blue, big, funny, tall or square.
>
> Or **which one** – this, that, first, last or other.
>
> Or **how many** – one, many, some, three or each.

Read these sentences. Underline the adjectives.

① The girls played in the shade of the big tree.

② The yellow duck won the race.

③ The children laughed at the funny clown.

④ The tiny frog jumped onto the log.

⑤ Three boys rode their bikes to the beach.

Choose adjectives from the list to complete the sentences. Some will be left over.

each
happy
huge
last
late
tasty
shady
tall
wrong

⑥ The _____ children played at the beach.

⑦ They made a _____ sandcastle.

⑧ They splashed _____ other with the water.

⑨ They ate a _____ lunch in the shade.

⑩ They went home when it was _____ afternoon.

Write each adjective in the box beside the best noun.

broken	enormous	excited	fast	red

⑪ _____ hen

⑫ _____ car

⑬ _____ toy

⑭ _____ elephant

⑮ _____ puppy

Score 2 points for each correct answer!

SCORE **/30** (0-12) (14-24) (26-30)

TARGETING HOMEWORK 1 © PASCAL PRESS ISBN 9781925726435

Syllables

Words are made up of **syllables**. You can **clap the syllables** in words.

Some words have **one syllable (one clap)**: cat plane book shoe

Some words have **two syllables**: rabbit donut window peanut

These words have **three syllables**: butterfly alphabet spaghetti

This word has **four syllables**: caterpillar

Every syllable must have a **vowel sound**.

Remember that some **vowel sounds** have more than one letter (like **ai**, **ea** and **igh**). Sometimes the letters are separated, as in **plane** – the vowel sound is made of the **a** and the **e** at the end.

Underline the **vowel sounds** in these words. Write the number of syllables. Clap the words to help.

1. pot ____ syllable
2. pumpkin ____ syllables
3. super ____ syllables
4. tomato ____ syllables
5. crocodile ____ syllables

6. cane ____ syllable
7. hammer ____ syllables
8. happy ____ syllables
9. strawberry ____ syllables
10. supermarket ____ syllables

It is easier to spell **long words** when you know how to break them into **syllables**.

Read the words. Show how you could break them into syllables.

11. hundred = _____ + _____
12. picnic = _____ + _____
13. butter = _____ + _____

14. rocket = _____ + _____
15. bedroom = _____ + _____
16. sorry = _____ + _____

Look at the pictures. Write the words. Break them into syllables to help.

17. _____

19. _____

18. _____

Score 2 points for each correct answer!

SCORE **/38** (0-16) (18-32) (34-38)

Trace the words. Start at the star. Follow the arrows.

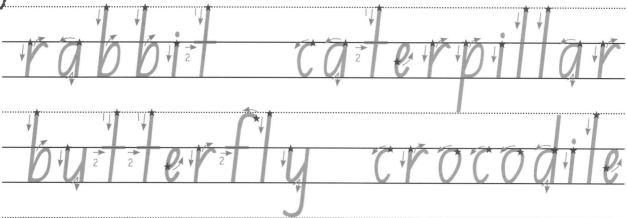

TERM 4 ENGLISH

Reading & Comprehension

AC9E1LY01, AC9E1LY05

Imaginative text – Narrative

The Beach Surprise

Nala and Jack went to the beach.

"Let's make a sandcastle," said Nala.

"Yes," said Jack. "Let's make it here near the water."

"No," said Nala. "The waves will wash it away. Let's make it up near the dunes."

The children made a big sandcastle.

"Our sandcastle needs a flag," said Jack.

"Our sandcastle needs a door and some windows," said Nala. "Let's find some shells."

The children found some shells. They took them back to the sandcastle.

They put the shells on the sandcastle.

"Look!" said Jack.

Nala looked.

One of the windows was moving.

"Oh!" the children laughed.

"That window has a crab inside."

TARGETING HOMEWORK 1 © PASCAL PRESS ISBN 9781925726435

Write or circle the correct answers.

① Where did the children go?

☐ **a** to a farm

☐ **b** to the beach

☐ **c** home

② What did the children make?

☐ **a** a sandcastle

☐ **b** a cake

☐ **c** a house

③ Where did the children make the sandcastle?

☐ **a** in the water

☐ **b** near the water

☐ **c** up near the dunes

④ What did the children use for doors and windows?

☐ **a** blocks   ☐ **b** shells   ☐ **c** crabs

⑤ What gave the children a surprise?

☐ **a** a crab

☐ **b** the water

☐ **c** the sand

⑥ How do you think the children felt when they saw the window move?

☐ **a** frightened

☐ **b** proud

☐ **c** amused

⑦ What were the names of the children?

_____

_____

⑧ Who had the idea to make a sandcastle?

_____

⑨ Why did the children make the sandcastle near the dunes?

☐ **a** So it wouldn't wash away.

☐ **b** So they could make it bigger.

☐ **c** So the crabs wouldn't get it.

⑩ What do you think the children used for a flag?

_____

Score 2 points for each correct answer!   **SCORE**   **/20**   (0-8)   (10-14)   (16-20)

TERM 4 ENGLISH

My Book Review

Title _____

Author _____

Colour stars to show your rating: ☆ ☆ ☆ ☆ ☆

Boring   Great!

Comment _____

_____

Numbers more than 100

① Starting at 100, count the number of blocks by ones. Write the numbers.

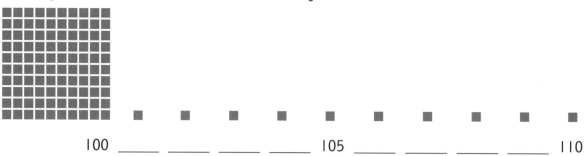

100 _____ _____ _____ _____ 105 _____ _____ _____ _____ 110

② Starting at 100, count the number of blocks by twos. Write the numbers.

100   102   _____ _____ _____ 110   112   _____ _____

③ Starting at one hundred, count in fives. Write the numbers.

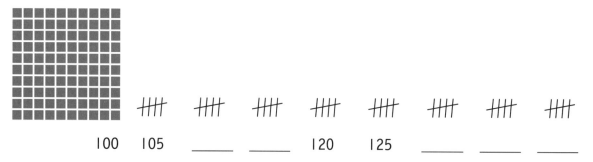

100   105   _____ _____ 120   125   _____ _____ _____

④ Look at the number line. Write the missing numbers.

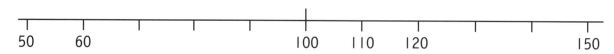

Look at these blocks. Write how many you see.

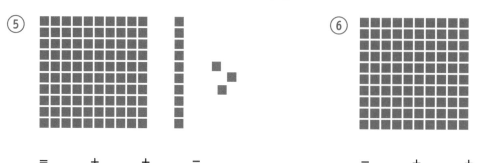

⑤ = ____ + ____ + ____ = ____

⑥ = ____ + ____ + ____ = ____

TARGETING HOMEWORK 1 © PASCAL PRESS ISBN 9781925726435

Read these number stories. Draw the picture in the box. Write the number fact.

⑦ The salesman had 6 cars.
He sold 3 cars.
How many cars are left?

_____

⑧ The children baked 12 cookies.
They took 6 cookies to school.
How many were left at home?

_____

⑨ Tan had 8 coins.
Jodie had 5 coins.
How many more coins did Tan have?

_____

⑩ Jaz made 7 paper planes.
Zara made 3 paper planes.
How many planes did they have
altogether?

_____

Money

Count the money in these money boxes. Write how much.

⑪ _____

⑬ _____

⑫ _____

⑭ _____

TERM 4 MATHS

Draw lines to match the coins to the objects they can buy.

⑮

⑰

 $3

 $2

 $4

 $7

⑯

⑱

⑲ Circle the object that costs the most money.

Score 2 points for each correct answer! **SCORE** **/38** (0-16) (18-32) (34-38)

Statistics

AC9M1ST01

Data representation

The children counted the colours of cars that passed by the school. They used tallies to count.

car	I
car	ﷻ ﷻ
car	ﷻ III
car	IIII
car	ﷻ

TARGETING HOMEWORK 1 © PASCAL PRESS ISBN 9781925726435

① Show your information on the graph.

Colours of Cars That Passed by School

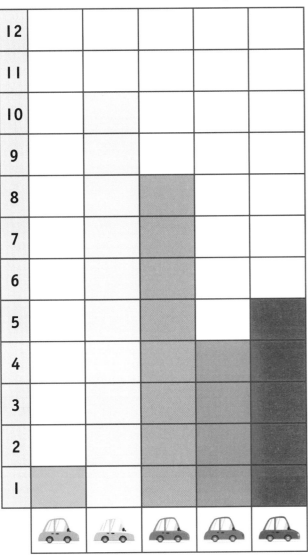

12					
11					
10					
9					
8					
7					
6					
5					
4					
3					
2					
1					

Answer these questions.

② Which colour car did the children see most? _____

③ How many blue cars did they see? _____

④ Which colour car did the children see least? _____

⑤ How many cars did the children see altogether? _____

⑥ Did they see more yellow cars or more grey cars? _____

⑦ How many more? _____

⑧ How many red cars did the children see? _____

⑨ Did the children see more red cars or more blue cars? _____

⑩ How many more? _____

TERM 4 MATHS

Score 2 points for each correct answer!

SCORE | / 20 | 0-8 | 10-14 | 16-20

AC9M1N01

Problem Solving

Can you solve these Sudoku puzzles?

You may only use the numbers 1, 2, 3 and 4.
The numbers 1, 2, 3, and 4 must appear in each row, in each column and in each red box.

		2	
	4		1
	3	4	
4			

1		4	
	2		3
3			
		1	4

Adjectives — opposites

Some **adjectives** are **opposites**.
Big is the opposite of **small**. **Happy** is the opposite of **sad**.

Choose the opposites from the box.

① **Enormous** is the opposite of _____.

② **Many** is the opposite of _____.

③ **Left** is the opposite of _____.

④ **Right** is the opposite of _____.

⑤ **First** is the opposite of _____.

⑥ **Healthy** is the opposite of _____.

⑦ **Fast** is the opposite of _____.

⑧ **Short** is the opposite of _____.

⑨ **Hot** is the opposite of _____.

cold
few
last
right
sick
slow
tall
tiny
wrong

Sometimes we put **un** in front of a word to make the **opposite**.
For example, **unhappy** means sad or not happy.

Write un in front of these words to make the opposite. Write the meanings.

⑩ _____lucky means _____.

⑪ _____kind means _____.

⑫ _____afraid means _____.

⑬ _____fair means _____.

⑭ _____well means _____.

⑮ _____tidy means _____.

⑯ _____safe means _____.

⑰ _____healthy means _____.

⑱ _____used means _____.

Score 2 points
for each
correct answer!

SCORE

/36   (0-16)   (18-30)   (32-36)

Compound words

> **Compound words** are special words that are made up of **two smaller words.**
> For example, **bedroom** is made up of **bed** and **room.**

Read these compound words. Write the two smaller words they are made from.

① butterfly = _____ + _____

② cupcake = _____ + _____

③ railroad = _____ + _____

Write the compound word that is made from these two words.
Be careful! The two words are not always in the right order.

④ bow + rain = _____

⑤ cake + pan = _____

⑥ eye + ball = _____

Choose a word from the box to make a compound word.

ball	day	port	trap
corn	fire	shine	worm

⑦ mouse_____

⑧ camp_____

⑨ birth_____

⑩ earth_____

⑪ sun_____

⑫ air_____

⑬ foot_____

⑭ pop_____

Trace the words. Start at the star. Follow the arrows.

hamburger eyeball

snowman raincoat

Score 2 points for each correct answer!

SCORE **/28** 0-12 14-22 24-28

TERM 4 ENGLISH

Imaginative text – Narrative

Little Koala's Party

"Let's have a party," said Little Koala.

"Yes," said Mother Koala. "We will invite all our friends."

Little Koala made a list of all their friends. She wrote down how many in each family.

> Kangaroo Family — 3
> Emu Family — 5
> Wombat Family — 4
> Echidna Family — 6

"Did you forget someone?" asked Mother Koala.

Little Koala looked at the list. All her friends were there.

"What about us?" asked Mother Koala.

"Oops," said Little Koala. She added them to the list, Koala Family – 3.

"How many is that?" asked Father Koala. "Twenty-one," said Little Koala. "There will be 21 at our party, including us!"

Little Koala wrote the invitations to her friends:

> Dear Joey,
>
> Please come to my party, at my home on Saturday, at 2 o'clock.
>
> Please bring all your family.
> It will be fun.
>
> From Little Koala

Then the Koala family got ready for the party. They made two gumleaf pies, one wattle cupcake and one glass of bush punch for each guest. Little Koala made sure there were pies, cupcakes and drinks for them too.

When Saturday came, they all had a wonderful party.

TARGETING HOMEWORK 1 © PASCAL PRESS ISBN 9781925726435

Write or circle the correct answers.

① Who wanted to have a party?

- ☐ **a** Little Koala
- ☐ **b** Little Kangaroo
- ☐ **c** Father Koala

② Which of these families were not invited to the party?

- ☐ **a** Kangaroo
- ☐ **b** Snake
- ☐ **c** Wombat

③ Who did Little Koala forget to add to the list?

_____

④ How many are in the Kangaroo family?

_____

⑤ Which family has the most?

_____

⑥ What day is the party?

_____

⑦ What time is the party?

- ☐ **a** 10 am
- ☐ **b** 2 pm
- ☐ **c** 6 pm

⑧ What did the Koala family **not** serve at the party?

- ☐ **a** gumleaf pies
- ☐ **b** wattle cupcakes
- ☐ **c** gumnut crackers

⑨ What drink did the Koala family serve at the party?

- ☐ **a** bush lemonade
- ☐ **b** bush punch
- ☐ **c** bush coffee

⑩ How many cupcakes were needed for the party?

- ☐ **a** 3
- ☐ **b** 21
- ☐ **c** 42

TERM 4 ENGLISH

Score 2 points for each correct answer!

SCORE **/20** (0-8) (10-14) (16-20)

My Book Review

Title _____

Author _____

Colour stars to show your rating: ☆ ☆ ☆ ☆ ☆

Boring   Great!

Comment _____

_____

Number & Algebra

AC9M1N01, AC9M1N02, AC9M1N03, AC9M1N04, AC9M1N05, AC9M1N06, AC9M1A01, AC9M1A02

Numbers more than 100

Look at these hundreds, tens and one. Write how many altogether.

TERM 4 MATHS

①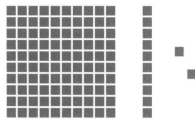

___ hundreds, ___ tens and ___ ones

= _____

②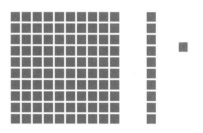

___ hundreds, ___ tens and ___ ones

= _____

③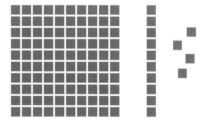

___ hundreds, ___ tens and ___ ones

= _____

④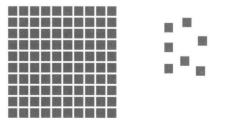

___ hundreds, ___ tens and ___ ones

= _____

⑤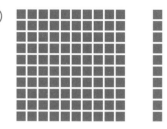

___ hundreds, ___ tens and ___ ones

= _____

⑥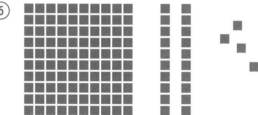

___ hundreds, ___ tens and ___ ones

= _____

⑦

___ hundreds, ___ tens and ___ ones

= _____

⑧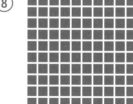

___ hundreds, ___ tens and ___ ones

= _____

TARGETING HOMEWORK 1 © PASCAL PRESS ISBN 9781925726435

Draw hundreds, tens and ones to show these numbers.

⑨ **86**

⑪ **109**

⑩ **115**

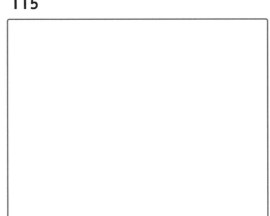

⑫ **121**

Write the missing numbers in these patterns.

⑬ 25, 30, 35, _____, _____, _____, _____, 60, _____.

I am counting in _____.

⑭ 75, 80, 85, _____, _____, _____, 105, _____.

I am counting in _____.

⑮ 100, 102, 104, _____, _____, _____, 112, _____.

I am counting in _____.

⑯ 70, 80, 90, _____, _____, _____, 130, _____.

I am counting in _____.

⑰ 98, 99, 100, _____, _____, _____, 104, _____.

I am counting in _____.

⑱ 106, 105, 104, _____, _____, _____, 100, _____.

I am counting in _____.

Number & Algebra

Draw tens to show these add stories. Write how many altogether.

⑲ Tema had 5 towers of ten.
Tan had 4 towers of ten.
How many blocks did they have altogether?

Draw the tens here:

⑳ Sam had 4 towers of ten.
Sarah had 3 towers of ten.
How many blocks did they have altogether?

Draw the tens here:

_____ + _____ = _____

_____ + _____ = _____

Making equal groups

Tema was counting his $2 coins. He put them into groups of 5.

㉑ Circle groups of 5 coins.

㉒ How many coins does Tema have altogether? _____

㉓ How many coins are in each group? _____

㉔ How many groups did Tema make? _____

Sarah was counting her 50 cent coins. She put them into groups of 2.

㉕ Circle groups of 2 coins.

㉖ How many coins does Sarah have altogether? _____

㉗ How many coins are in each group? _____

㉘ How many groups did Sarah make? _____

TARGETING HOMEWORK 1 © PASCAL PRESS ISBN 9781925726435

Hana put her toy cars in rows.

㉙ Circle each row of cars.

㉚ How many cars does
Hana have altogether? _____

㉛ How many cars are in each row? _____

㉜ How many rows did Hana make? _____

Look at Li's garden beds.

㉝ How many flowers does Li have altogether? _____

㉞ How many flowers are in each garden bed? _____

㉟ How many garden beds did Li make? _____

Repeating patterns

What comes next? Circle the part of the pattern that repeats. Continue the patterns.

㊱  _____ _____

㊲ dog, cat, pig, dog, dog, cat, pig, dog, dog, cat, pig, _____, _____

㊳ 1, 1, 2, 1, 1, 2, 1, 1, ____, ____

Score 2 points
for each
correct answer!

SCORE /76 (0-34) (34-70) (72-76)

Problem Solving

AC9M1N01, AC9M1N04

Can you solve this magic square?

When it is finished, it will have all the numbers
1, 2, 3, 4, 5, 6, 7, 8 and 9.

The numbers in every row, every column and
both diagonals will add to 15.

Start with the middle square.
It is the easiest number to find.

Use this number line to help you with your additions.

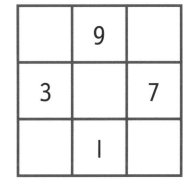

	9	
3		7
	1	

| 1 | 2 | 3 | 4 | 5 | 6 | 7 | 8 | 9 | 10 | 11 | 12 | 13 | 14 | 15 | 16 | 17 | 18 | 19 | 20 |

Grammar & Punctuation

Choose verbs from the box to complete these sentences.

① Horses _____ fast.

② Dolphins _____ in the ocean.

③ Snakes _____ in the grass.

④ Kangaroos _____.

⑤ Koalas _____ gum leaves.

⑥ Cockatoos _____ loudly.

eat
gallop
jump
slither
squawk
swim

Cross out the incorrect verb in these sentences.

⑦ The bus (stops / stop) at this corner every day.

⑧ Ali and Jacob (is / are) best friends.

⑨ I (were / am) hungry!

⑩ We (will ask /asks) if we can go to the beach tomorrow.

⑪ Kali (rode / ride) her new scooter to school.

Choose adjectives from the box to complete these sentences.

busy	first	funny	shady	untidy
dirty	five	scary	unhappy	

⑫ Sarah looked both ways before crossing the _____ road.

⑬ The _____ puppy cried at the door.

⑭ It took a long time to clean his room because he was so _____.

⑮ Max's poster was the best so he won _____ prize.

⑯ There are _____ players on the netball team.

⑰ The _____ monster in the play frightened the children.

⑱ The children laughed at the _____ clown.

⑲ The girls washed their _____ hands before they ate lunch.

⑳ The family sat under the _____ tree in the park.

Score 2 points for each correct answer!

SCORE **/40** (0-18) (20-34) (36-40)

TARGETING HOMEWORK 1 © PASCAL PRESS ISBN 9781925726435

Phonic Knowledge & Spelling

Vowel sounds

Read these words. Circle the word with a **different vowel sound**.

① cat apple wash hand

② cot come top rod

③ bit ride bike fly

④ rid fly night pie

⑤ blow gone so bone

⑥ cup put sun but

⑦ me see met seat

⑧ eight snail plane mat

⑨ thief key night leap

⑩ blew blue belt pool

Syllables

Underline the **vowels** in these words. Then complete the table.

	Word	Number of syllables	Syllables
⑪	gallop		+
⑫	flipper		+
⑬	butter		+
⑭	happy		+
⑮	chicken		+

Choose words from the box to make compound words.

board	day	fast	print	shine

⑯ foot_____

⑰ sun_____

⑱ birth_____

⑲ break_____

⑳ skate_____

Score 2 points for each correct answer! **SCORE** **/40** (0-18) (20-34) (36-40)

Number & Algebra

Look at these hundreds, tens and ones. Write how many altogether.

①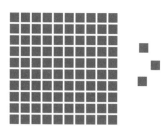

___ hundreds, ___ tens and ___ ones

= _____

③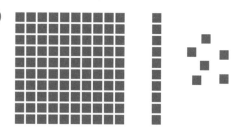

___ hundreds, ___ tens and ___ ones

= _____

②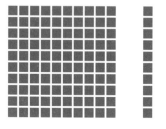

___ hundreds, ___ tens and ___ ones

= _____

④

___ hundreds, ___ tens and ___ ones

= _____

Continue these counting patterns. Explain how you are counting.

⑤
88	90	92	94								

I am counting in _____.

⑥
65	70	75	80								

I am counting in _____.

⑦
65	67	69	71								

I am counting in _____.

⑧
30	40	50	60								

I am counting in _____.

⑨
95	96	97	98								

I am counting in _____.

TARGETING HOMEWORK 1 © PASCAL PRESS ISBN 9781925726435

TERM 4 MATHS

Read these number stories. Draw the picture in the box. Write the number fact.

⑩ Tema had 9 marbles.
5 rolled away.
How many marbles are left?

_____

⑪ Jaz had 8 butterflies.
She gave 3 to Zara.
How many butterflies does Jaz have now?

_____

⑫ Jodie and Tan made 12 cupcakes.
They ate 4.
How many cupcakes are left?

_____

⑬ Tema had 4 marbles. Tan had 5 marbles.
How many marbles did they have
altogether?

_____

Score 2 points for each correct answer!   SCORE /26   (0-10) (12-20) (22-26)

Measurement & Space

ACMMG019, ACMMG022

Time

Draw lines to match the clocks to the times.

①    ②    ③    ④

| 6 o'clock | half past 1 | half past 10 | 4 o'clock |

Score 2 points for each correct answer!   SCORE /8   (0-2) (4-6) (8)

MY READING LIST

Name: _____

_____

	Title	Author	Rating	Date
1			☆☆☆☆☆	
2			☆☆☆☆☆	
3			☆☆☆☆☆	
4			☆☆☆☆☆	
5			☆☆☆☆☆	
6			☆☆☆☆☆	
7			☆☆☆☆☆	
8			☆☆☆☆☆	
9			☆☆☆☆☆	
10			☆☆☆☆☆	
11			☆☆☆☆☆	
12			☆☆☆☆☆	
13			☆☆☆☆☆	
14			☆☆☆☆☆	
15			☆☆☆☆☆	
16			☆☆☆☆☆	
17			☆☆☆☆☆	
18			☆☆☆☆☆	
19			☆☆☆☆☆	
20			☆☆☆☆☆	
21			☆☆☆☆☆	
22			☆☆☆☆☆	
23			☆☆☆☆☆	
24			☆☆☆☆☆	
25			☆☆☆☆☆	
26			☆☆☆☆☆	
27			☆☆☆☆☆	
28			☆☆☆☆☆	
29			☆☆☆☆☆	
30			☆☆☆☆☆	
31			☆☆☆☆☆	
32			☆☆☆☆☆	

TARGETING HOMEWORK 1 © PASCAL PRESS ISBN 9781925726435

Unit 1 ENGLISH: Grammar & Punctuation

1 Answers will vary – child's name
2 Answers will vary – child's gender
3 Answers will vary – child's age
4 Answers will vary – what child likes to do
5 Answers will vary – child's favourite colour
6 Answers will vary – child's favourite food
7 The dog ran after the stick.
8 A book is on the table.
9 The girl has a pet cat.
10 A monkey is in the tree.

Unit 1 ENGLISH: Phonic Knowledge & Spelling

1 pen
2 jam
3 truck
4 zip
5 king
6 fox
7 cat
8 nest
9 duck
10 bug
11 jam
12 pig
13 zip

Unit 1 ENGLISH: Reading & Comprehension

1 At a billabong
2 a bullfrog
3 two pelicans
4 three turtles
5 four crayfish
6 five platypuses
7 no one
8 a crocodile
9 b It heard all the noise.
10 c The crocodile ate them.

Unit 2 MATHS: Number & Algebra

1 6
2 9
3 7
4 8
5 9
6 15
7 11
8 4, 8, 9
9 7, 10, 11, 12
10 10, 12, 14, 16, 18, 20
11 10, 15, 20
12 8 objects
13 13 objects
14 2 and 3 makes 5
15 6 and 5 makes 11
16 Draw: ▮   Circle: ⬤

17 Draw: ☺   Circle: ☺ ♥
18 Draw: ▮   Circle: ▮ ▮ ▲

Unit 2 MATHS: Measurement & Space

2 Items longer than 6 cm are blue: pencil, paintbrush, ruler, marker, spoon
3 Items shorter than 6 cm are red: safety pin, eraser, screw
4 Answers will vary; the object should be longer than 6 cm.
5 Answers will vary; the object should be shorter than 6 cm.

6–9

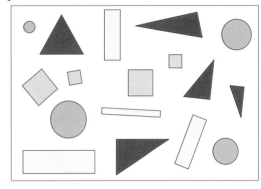

Unit 3 ENGLISH: Grammar & Punctuation

1 The little boy [ran] to his father.
2 The sun shone [shone] in the morning.
3 The strong woman [lifted] the heavy car.
4 The big dog [jumped] very high.
5 The baby cried [cried] because he was hungry.
6 to his father
7 very high
8 in the morning
9 because he was hungry
10 the heavy car
11 Yes. The hungry girl ate the red apple.
12 No
13 No
14 Yes. The kangaroo jumped over the fence.
15 Yes. The children ran across the park.

Unit 3 ENGLISH: Phonic Knowledge & Spelling

1 cake
2 gate
3 five
4 snake
5 ripe
6 pipe
7 bike
8 pine
9 tape
10 cane

Unit 3 ENGLISH: Reading & Comprehension

1 a. to help us find our way around
2 stop
3 b. airport sign
4 a. a walk light
5 b. Listen for beeps at the crossing.
6 a. information sign
7 an open sign on a toy shop

Unit 4 MATHS: Number & Algebra

1 8
2 15
3 12
4 8
5 8
6 20
7 4, 5, 7, 8, 9
8 2, 4, 6, 8, 10, 12, 14
9 10, 20, 30, 40, 50, 60, 70, 80, 90, 100
10 9 triangles
11 19 circles
12 5 and 4 makes 9
13 4 and 3 makes 7
14 6 and 2 makes 8
15 5 and 5 makes 10
16 7
17 7

Unit 4 MATHS: Measurement & Space

1 Longest time: A tree grows.
  Shortest time: Blow out candles.
2 Longest time: Build a house.
  Shortest time: Eat an icecream.
3 Get dressed.
4 Bake the cake.
5–10 Left hands are coloured blue, right hands are coloured red

Unit 4 MATHS: Problem solving

1 apple
2 bone
3 treasure chest
4 ball
5 The most direct ways are:
  Down 4 squares then right 4 squares.
  OR Right 4 squares then down 4 squares.
  Other more indirect answers are possible.

Unit 5 ENGLISH: Grammar & Punctuation

1 The farmer
2 milked
3 the cow
4 The children ate the birthday cake.
5 The dog hurt its paw.
6 The ball flew over the fence.
7 The bird sang loudly.
8 when
9 where
10 how
11 why

12 The kitten chased the ball.
13 A bee was on the flower.
14 The children played games after lunch.

Unit 5 ENGLISH: Phonic Knowledge & Spelling

1 note
2 cute
3 cube
4 hope
5 rope
6 rule
7 robe
8 rose
9 cute
10 rude

Unit 5 ENGLISH: Reading & Comprehension

1 b. All bees are insects.
2 c. 6
3 a. You can see through them.
4 c. in a hive
5 b. no
6 b. on their legs
7 c. honey and pollen
8 a. nectar
9 They give us honey. They help fruit and vegetables to grow.

Unit 6 MATHS: Number & Algebra

1 11
2 14
3 17
4 7
5 11
6 16
7 10
8 19
9 14
10 13
11 10
12 17
13 8, 10, 14, 18
14 7, 13, 15
15 5, 10, 15, 20
16 The number squares 10, 20, 30, 40, 50, 60, 70, 80, 90, 100 should be coloured.
17 10, 20, 30, 40, 50, 60, 70, 80, 90, 100
18 7
19 6
20 5
21 6
22 50c
23 5c
24 $2
25 5c
26 4 coins, $2 is circled
27 6 coins, 50c is circled

TARGETING HOMEWORK 1 © PASCAL PRESS ISBN 9781925726435

Unit 6 MATHS: Statistics

1 6
2 3
3 9
4 the number of children who have a pet dog
5 A smiley face should be drawn in one of the columns.

Unit 6 MATHS: Problem Solving

5

Unit 7 ENGLISH: Grammar & Punctuation

1 Who played football?
2 What did the girls play?
3 Where did the girls play?
4 When did the girls play?
5 S
6 Q
7 Q
8 Q
9 S
10 Q

Unit 7 ENGLISH: Phonic Knowledge & Spelling

1 plane
2 paint
3 day
4 rain
5 way
6 beak
7 seal
8 feet
9 bee
10 seed

Unit 7 ENGLISH: Reading & Comprehension

1 c. the cat's face
2 3
3 the moon, sometimes
4 c. 6
5 a. ears
6 to stick it all together
7 c. whiskers
8 b. a cardboard circle
9 c. whiskers
10 Answers will vary – cat's name

Unit 8 MATHS: Number & Algebra

1 5
2 18
3 10
4 15
5 9
6 11
7 16
8 12
9 7
10 b. in 2s
11 10, 15, 20
12 10

13 6, draw 6 objects.
14 4, draw 4 objects.
15 10, draw 10 objects.
16 3 + 4 = 7. Total = 7.
17 Answers will vary. Total = 6.
18 Answers will vary. Total = 8.
19 5
20 There should be 3 lollies in each box.
21 3
22 3
23 3
24 There should be 6 blocks in each box.
25 6
26 6
27 6

Unit 8 MATHS: Measurement & Space

1 Cross: elephant, lawnmower, couch, tiger
2 Circle: dice, tennis racquet, basketball, pasta meal, bicycle, baby
3 refrigerator
4 paperclip

Unit 8 MATHS: Problem Solving

horse

TERM 1 REVIEW

Term 1 ENGLISH: Grammar & Punctuation

1 The duck [swam] in the pond.
2 The bee [flew] from flower to flower.
3 The bird [hurt] its wing.
4 The children [played] in the rain.
5 S
6 Q
7 Q
8 S
9 The frog sat on the log.
10 When are we going home?
11 Why did the dog bark?
12 My friend is a fast runner.
13 Answers will vary.
14 Answers will vary.
15 Answers will vary.

Term 1 ENGLISH: Phonic Knowledge & Spelling

1 bug
2 peg
3 bat
4 fish
5 mop
6 pine
7 rope
8 cute
9 feet
10 cape
11 bike
12 cute
13 time

14 cake
15 rode, bike
16 team, game
17 paint, snail
18 shines, day

Term 1 MATHS: Number & Algebra

1–20

Numbers	Pictures	Tallies
1	●		
2	●●	||
3	●●●	|||
4	●●●●	||||
5	●●●●●	卌
6	●●●●●●	卌	
7	●●●●●●●	卌 ||
8	●●●●●●●●	卌 |||
9	●●●●●●●●●	卌 ||||
10	●●●●●●●●●●	卌 卌
11	●●●●●●●●●●●	卌 卌	
12	●●●●●●●●●●●●	卌 卌 ||
13	●●●●●●●●●●●●●	卌 卌 |||
14	●●●●●●●●●●●●●●	卌 卌 ||||
15	●●●●●●●●●●●●●●●	卌 卌 卌
16	●●●●●●●●●●●●●●●●	卌 卌 卌	
17	●●●●●●●●●●●●●●●●●	卌 卌 卌 ||
18	●●●●●●●●●●●●●●●●●●	卌 卌 卌 |||
19	●●●●●●●●●●●●●●●●●●●	卌 卌 卌 ||||
20	●●●●●●●●●●●●●●●●●●●●	卌 卌 卌 卌

21 3 + 4 = 7
22 6 + 1 = 7
23 9, 9 objects
24 7, 7 objects

Unit 9 ENGLISH: Grammar & Punctuation

1 The teacher sat <u>at his desk</u>.
2 Where did the teacher sit?
3 The teacher sat at his desk.
4 <u>The girl</u> swam in the river.
5 Who swam in the river?
6 The girl swam in the river.
7 C
8 0

9 0
10 C

Unit 9 ENGLISH: Phonic Knowledge & Spelling

1 made
2 cute
3 robe
4 kite
5 rain, day, snail, paint, pay
6 beet, seat, sheep, bean, seal
7 coat, boat, road, toad, soap
8 seal
9 snail
10 goat
11 boat, coat, float, moat
12 see, tree, knee, fee
13 make, lake, fake, bake

Unit 9 ENGLISH: Reading & Comprehension

1 b. a poem
2 a. asks a question.
3 b. choose
4 sea
5 under the sea?
6 climb in a tree?
7 Answers will vary, e.g. giraffe, elephant
8 Answers will vary, e.g. cheetah, antelope
9 Answers will vary, e.g. tortoise, caterpillar
10 me

Unit 10 MATHS: Measurement & Space

1 longer
2 shorter
3 longer
4 same
5 same
6 shorter
7 shorter

Unit 10 MATHS: Number & Algebra

2 2, 4, 6, 8, 10, 12, 14, 16, 18, 20, 22, 24, 26, 28, 30
4 20, 21, 22, 23, 24, 25, 26, 27, 28, 29, 30
5 5, 10, 15, 20, 25, 30
7 10, 20, 30, 40, 50, 60, 70, 80, 90, 100
8 10, 20, 30, 40, 50, 60, 70, 80, 90, 100
9 3 bags are circled, 3
10 3
11 3, 3
12 5, 2, 3
13 7, 3, 4

Unit 10 MATHS: Measurement & Space

1 Cubes are blue.
2 Spheres are red.
3 Cylinders are yellow.
4 Cones are green.
5 Rectangular prisms are purple.
6 cone
7 sphere
8 rectangular prism

9 cube
10 cylinder
11 Answers will vary, e.g. a dice.
12 Answers will vary, e.g. can of baked beans.
13 Answer will vary, e.g. cereal box.
14 Answers will vary, e.g. a ball.
15 Answers will vary, e.g. a witch's hat.
16 bucket
17 pink mug
18 Answers will vary, e.g. saucepan, bucket.
19 Answers will vary, e.g. medicine glass, spoon.

Unit 10 MATHS: Problem Solving

Answers will vary.

Unit 11 ENGLISH: Grammar & Punctuation

1 C
2 O
3 C
4 C
5 C
6 C
7 R
8 O
9 R
10 O
11 ?
12 !
13 ?
14 .
15 .

Unit 11 ENGLISH: Phonic Knowledge & Spelling

1 shine
2 show
3 shell
4 shed
5 bush
6 wish
7 push
8 cash
9 wish
10 shot
11 bush
12 shirt
13 chin
14 chop
15 cheer
16 chart
17 rich
18 munch
19 teach
20 march
21 couch
22 chick
23 child
24 bunch

Unit 11 ENGLISH: Reading & Comprehension

1 a. the child's grandmother
2 c. in the holidays
3 a. excited
4 b. insects
5 a. butterflies
6 honey
7 b. On Saturday
8 He was player of the match.
9 c. Ash's cousins.
10 He wants to play with his cousins.

Unit 12 MATHS: Number & Algebra

1

1	2	3	4	5	6	7	8	9	10
11	12	13	14	15	16	17	18	19	20
21	22	23	24	25	26	27	28	29	30
31	32	33	34	35	36	37	38	39	40

2 14
3 29
4 20
5 40
6 28
7 11
8 24
9 37
10 13
11 ||||| ||||| ||||| ||||| ||||| ||||| ||||| |||||
12 10, 20, 30, 40
13 6 + 4 = 10
14 3 + 2 = 5
15 4 + 6 = 10
16 2 + 3 = 5
17 4
18 6
19 4
20 3

Unit 12 MATHS: Measurement & Space

1 2 o'clock
2 1 o'clock
3 6 o'clock
4 9 o'clock
5 8 o'clock
6 4 o'clock
7 Clock shows 3 o'clock
8 Clock shows 6 o'clock
9 Clock shows 11 o'clock
10–12 Arrows show clockwise.

Unit 12 MATHS: Problem Solving

lizard

Unit 13 ENGLISH: Grammar & Punctuation

1 R
2 C
3 C
4 R
5 C
6 Will you play with me?
7 The children played in the playground.
8 Go and stand by the door.
9 Can you open this jar please?

Unit 13 ENGLISH: Phonic Knowledge & Spelling

1 thank
2 thin
3 thick
4 thirteen
5 with
6 both
7 sloth
8 path
9 feather
10 mother
11 weather
12 mother
13 bother
14 then
15 feather
16 mouth, tooth, feather, 30

Unit 13 ENGLISH: Reading & Comprehension

1 c. the child's grandfather
2 b. He sent an email every night.
3 c. a pod of dolphins
4 a. white
5 huge piles of icecream
6 b. The boat had a glass bottom.
7 b. on the ice
8 5
9 amazing
10 c. Take the child to Antarctica

Unit 14 MATHS: Number & Algebra

1 10, 20, 30, 40, 50
2 5
3 50
4 7
5 4
6 6
7 2
8 4
9 5
10 5, 6, 8, 9, 11, 12, 13, 15, 16, 17, 18, 19
11 17
12 14
13 16
14 $7 - 3 = 4$
15 $6 - 3 = 3$
16 $8 - 4 = 4$
17 $5 - 3 = 2$
18 Answers will vary.

19 50c
20 5c
21 $2
22 50c
23 5c, 10c, 20c, 50c, $1, $2
24 6
25 9
26 Piggy bank with 9 dollar coins is circled.

Unit 14 MATHS: Statistics

1 tick, 14
2 tick, 9
3 cross
4 tick, 23
5 cross
6 tick, 5
7 Answers will vary, e.g. ride bikes, bus, car, train.

Unit 14 MATHS: Problem Solving

scooter

Unit 15 ENGLISH: Grammar & Punctuation

1 the ball
2 the girl
3 the children
4 Tia and Max went to the park. **They** took a ball with **them**. It was Tia's ball. **She** got **it** at the shops on Saturday. First, Tia kicked the ball to Max. Then Max kicked **it** back to Tia. **He** kicked **it** too far. Tia had to run after **it**. Then **she** kicked the ball back to Max. The children played all afternoon. Then **they** went home.
5 I
6 us
7 she
8 them
9 you, ?
10 it, !
11 I, .

Unit 15 ENGLISH: Phonic Knowledge & Spelling

1 dolphin
2 photo
3 phone
4 trophy
5 microphone
6 squid
7 question
8 quack
9 equals
10 queen

Unit 15 ENGLISH: Reading & Comprehension

1 b. a pet dog.
2 b. no
3 c. They make too much mess.
4 a. Dogs have to be walked.
5 c. Mum and Dad
6 b. false
7 Walking a dog is good exercise.
8 b. The children sleep better.
9 c. Wash the dishes
10 Answers will vary.

TARGETING HOMEWORK 1 © PASCAL PRESS ISBN 9781925726435

Unit 16 MATHS: Number & Algebra

1 10, 20, 30, 40, 50, 60
2 6
3 60
4 5, 10, 15, 20, 25, 30, 35, 40, 45, 50, 55, 60
5 14, 14 hearts
6 17, 17 hears
7 13, 13 hearts
8 14, ‖‖‖ ‖‖‖ ‖‖‖‖
9 16, ‖‖‖ ‖‖‖ ‖‖‖ ‖
10 18, ‖‖‖ ‖‖‖ ‖‖‖ ‖‖‖
11 7
12 3
13 7
14 3
15 8 + 2 = 10
16 10 – 2 = 8
17 5 + 5 = 10
18 10 – 5 = 5
19 6 + 4 = 10
20 10 – 4 = 6
21 9 + 1 = 10
22 10 – 1 = 9
23 Circle 4 groups of 3 cookies.
24 4 bags
25 Circle 5 pairs of 2 socks.
26 5 pairs
27 Circle 4 groups of 5 balloons
28 4 bunches
29 Circle 4 groups of 2 books.
30 4 prize winners

31 Repeat: 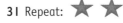 Draw:

32 Repeat:  Draw:

33 Repeat: Draw:

34 Repeat: **1 2 3** Draw: **3 1**

Unit 16 MATHS: Problem Solving

Answers will vary. Mathematically, you need to pull out 6 socks to be certain of getting a pair. But because this is a real-life experiment, it is possible to get a pair from taking out just two squares.

TERM 2 REVIEW

Term 2 ENGLISH: Grammar & Punctuation

1 Q
2 R
3 Q
4 C
5 S
6 S
7 C
8 R
9 0
10 C
11 0
12 C
13 C
14 0
15 Where did you put my scooter?
16 Stop that!
17 I forgot to bring my lunch.
18 they
19 I
20 we
21 us
22 them
23 we

Term 2 ENGLISH: Phonic Knowledge & Spelling

1 feet
2 cube
3 cane
4 tail
5 coat
6 ride
7 meat
8 day
9 tune
10 rope
11 ship
12 chop
13 wish
14 wash
15 chew
16 thing
17 both
18 thirteen
19 moth
20 think
21 question
22 phone
23 photo
24 quack

Term 2 MATHS: Number & Algebra

1 8, 15, 19, 22, 30, 36, 41, 47, 53, 54
2 Even number to 60 are coloured.
3 Multiples of 5 are circled.
4 Multiples of 10 are crossed.
5 d. They are all coloured, circled and crossed.
6 24, 26, 32, 34. 2s.
7 38, 39, 42, 43. 1s.
8 40, 50. 10s.
9 20, 25, 45, 50. 5s.
10 26
11 44
12 57
13 36
14 41
15 24
16 18
17 33
18 41
19 14

20 18

21 11

22 12

23 15

24 19

25 3

26 1

27 4 + 3 = 7

28 5 + 4 = 9

Term 2 MATHS: Measurement & Space

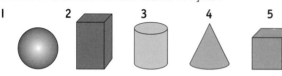

1   2   3   4   5

Unit 17 ENGLISH: Grammar & Punctuation

1 Answers will vary; e.g. my fat cat

2 Answers will vary; e.g. the huge chocolate cake

3 Answers will vary; e.g. a friendly bear

4 Answers will vary; e.g. this new game

5 The boy rode his new bike.

6 The green frog hopped into the water.

7 The children got onto the yellow bus.

8 The football team scored three goals.

9 Ari

10 Sydney

11 Stef, Angry Goose

12 Kakadu

Unit 17 ENGLISH: Phonic Knowledge & Spelling

1 wheel

2 whale

3 whistle

4 whisper

5 white

6 wheat

7 while

8 block

9 duck

10 kick

11 black

12 Jack

13 rock

14 lick

15 ring

16 sing

17 spring

Unit 17 ENGLISH: Reading & Comprehension

1 b. talking about their children

2 c. monkey

3 b. running

4 elephant

5 a. proud.

6 c. disappointed.

7 b. So their children could learn to do everything.

8 Answers will vary; e.g. because owls are wise.

9 b. no

10 a. You have to be the best at everything.

Unit 18 MATHS: Number & Algebra

1 These numbers are coloured blue: 20, 30, 40, 50, 60, 70, 80, 90, 100.

2 10, 20, 30, 40, 50, 60, 70, 80, 90, 100

3 These numbers are circled: 10, 15, 20, 25, 30, 35, 40, 45, 50, 55, 60, 65, 70, 75, 80, 85, 90, 95, 100.

4 These numbers are coloured green: 7, 17, 27, 37, 47, 57, 67, 70, 71, 72, 73, 74, 75, 76, 77, 78, 79, 87, 97.

5 Students should describe the shapes the see in the grid: a vertical straight line from 7 to 97, and a horizontal line from 71 to 79, and 70 by itself, up diagonally from 79.

6 58, 59, 61, 62. I am counting in 1s.

7 28, 32, 36. I am counting in 2s.

8 40, 45, 60. I am counting in 5s.

9 40, 50, 80. I am counting in 10s.

10 65

11 44

12 28

13 76

14 71

15 65

16 26

17 17

18 29

19 47

20 72

21 60

22 72

23 43

24 62

25 75

26 6

27 4

28 4 + 6 = 10, 6 + 4 = 10

29 9 + 1 = 10, 1 + 9 = 10

30 7 + 3 = 10, 3 + 7 = 10

31 8 + 2 + 10, 2 + 8 = 10

32 3

33 5

34 2

Unit 18 MATHS: Measurement & Space

1 Answers will vary.

2 Answers will vary.

3 approximately 7

4 approximately 6

5 approximately 5

6 approximately 8

7 Jodie

8 Mark

9 No - a different object will give different numbers, but the actual lengths stay the same.

10 Answers will vary. Students may notice that larger objects are less accurate, and it is difficult to measure around curves.

11 rectangle   **12** circle

13 square   **14** triangle

Unit 18 MATHS: Problem Solving

1 Matt
2 Tam
3 You would
4 fewer

Unit 19 ENGLISH: Grammar & Punctuation

1 two clocks
2 a pile of books
3 a pencil
4 a book
5 one clock
6 a tin of pencils
7 bikes
8 flowers
9 elephants
10 pencils
11 Thursday
12 Saturday
13 Monday
14 Friday
15 Tuesday
16 Sunday
17 Wednesday

Unit 19 ENGLISH: Phonic Knowledge & Spelling

1 pl
2 gl
3 bl
4 pl
5 cl
6 sl
7 bl
8 fl
9 blue
10 flower
11 blocks
12 glass
13 plane
14 slide
15 clock

Unit 19 ENGLISH: Reading & Comprehension

1 a. farm animals
2 llamas, camels
3 b. on farms in South America
4 b. clothes and blankets
5 c. Alpaca hair prickles like sheep's wool.
6 a. Alpaca hair can be dyed to make other colours.
7 b. a herd
8 gentle, friendly
9 c. grass and hay
10 c. three

Unit 20 MATHS: Number & Algebra

1 50
2 70
3 90
4 30
5 10
6 50
7 10
8 70
9 80
10 30
11 40
12 17
13 8, 18
14 10, fourteen
15 10, 6, sixteen
16 5, 10, 15, 20, 25, 30, 35, 40, 45, 50, 55, 60, 65, 70
17 2, 4, 6, 8, 10, 12, 14, 16, 18, 20, 22, 24, 26, 28
18 30, 31, 32, 33, 34, 35, 36, 37, 38, 39, 40, 41, 42, 43
19 26, 25, 24, 23, 22, 21, 20, 19, 18, 17, 16, 15, 14, 13
20 6
21 4
22 6 + 4 = 10
23 6
24 4
25 10 − 4 = 6 or 10 − 6 = 4
26 7 + 3 = 10 or 3 + 7 = 10
27 10 − 3 = 7 or 10 − 7 = 3
28 5 + 5 = 10
29 10 − 5 = 5
30 8 + 2 = 10 or 2 + 8 = 10
31 10 − 2 = 8 or 10 − 8 = 2
32 9 + 1 = 10 or 1 + 9 = 10
33 10 − 1 = 9 or 10 − 9 = 1

Unit 20 MATHS: Measurement & Space

1 August
2 31
3 Sunday
4 Tuesday
5 Weekend days are coloured.
6 4
7 5
8 3
9 Monday
10 Sunday
11 Mondays to Fridays are circled
12 22
13 9
14 Tuesdays
15 The path should follow the given directions.
16 Answers will vary.

Unit 20 MATHS: Problem Solving

1 Sunday   2 1 o'clock   3

ANSWERS

Unit 21 ENGLISH: Grammar & Punctuation

1. one dish
2. one peach
3. three boxes
4. four dresses
5. one box
6. two dishes
7. some peaches
8. a dress
9. spiders
10. crashes
11. torches
12. mixes
13. beaches
14. buses
15. June
16. October
17. December

Unit 21 ENGLISH: Phonic Knowledge & Spelling

1. br
2. cr
3. tr
4. fr
5. gr
6. tr
7. dr
8. pr
9. frog
10. present
11. bricks
12. train
13. grass
14. drum
15. crab

Unit 21 ENGLISH: Reading & Comprehension

1. yesterday
2. to look for minibeasts
3. c. a magnifying glass
4. b. to write about what they saw
5. b. four
6. c. see-through
7. b. from the flowers
8. blue with red spots
9. a. a lot
10. a. happy

Unit 22 MATHS: Number & Algebra

1. Colour 10, 20, 30, 40, 50, 60, 70, 80, 90, 100.
2. Circle 5, 10, 15, 20, 25, 30, 35, 40, 45, 50, 55, 60, 65, 70, 75, 80, 85, 90, 95, 100.
3. 22, 24, 26, 28, 30, 32, 34, 36, 38, 40, 42
4. Colour 42 red.
5. 64, 65, 66, 67, 68, 69, 70, 71, 72, 73, 74
6. Colour 74 yellow.
7. Colour 9, 19, 29, 39, 49, 59, 69, 79, 89, 90, 91, 92, 93, 94, 95, 96, 97, 98, 99 blue.
8. 34, 35, 36, 37, 38, 39
9. 58, 59, 60

10. 79, 80, 81
11. 7, 6, 5, 4, 3, 2, 1
12. 17, 16, 15, 14, 13, 12, 11, 10
13. 56, 55, 54, 53, 52, 51, 50
14. 73, 72, 71, 70, 69, 68, 67
15. Draw 7 buttons.
16. Draw 3 buttons.
17. Draw 3 buttons.
18. Draw 6 buttons.
19. 6 + 4 = 10
20. 5 + 2 = 7
21. 4 + 6 = 10
22. 2 + 5 = 7
23. Colour 20 coins.
24. 20
25. 20
26. Colour 10 coins.
27. 10
28. 10
29. Colour 5 coins.
30. 5
31. 5

Unit 22 MATHS: Statistics

1. ||||
2. |||| ||
3. ||||
4. |||| |

5.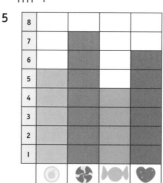

6.
7. (candy)
8. 7
9. (heart)
10. 1

Unit 22 MATHS: Problem Solving

6

Unit 23 ENGLISH: Grammar & Punctuation

1. feet
2. children
3. sheep
4. fish
5. mouse
6. people
7. women
8. teeth

TARGETING HOMEWORK 1 © PASCAL PRESS ISBN 9781925726435

9 Jacob, I

10 Susie, Mia

11 Lee, I

12 Sam, Zara

13 Nico

Unit 23 ENGLISH: Phonic Knowledge & Spelling

1 sw

2 sm

3 sn

4 st

5 sp

6 sp

7 sc

8 sk

9 scooter

10 twigs

11 snake

12 star

13 twins

14 swing

Unit 23 ENGLISH: Reading & Comprehension

1 b. a recipe.

2 c. how to make a sandwich.

3 a. things you need.

4 c. nutritious

5 a. butter

6 c. the eyes

7 b. the cheese

8 alfalfa hair

9 Eat it.

10 a. yes

Unit 24 MATHS: Number & Algebra

1 45

2 65

3 56

4 64

5 55

6 44

7 54

8 66

9 46

10 square

11 Circle 2, 12, 20, 21, 22, 23, 24, 25, 26, 27, 28, 29, 32, 42, 52, 62, 72, 82, 92.

12 2

13 3

14 4

15 5

16 6

17 7

18 8

19 9

20 $1 + 1 = 2$

21 $2 + 2 = 4$

22 $3 + 3 = 6$

23 $5 + 5 = 10$

24 $4 + 4 = 8$

25 $6 + 6 = 12$

26 $5 + 5 + 1 = 11$

27 $7 + 7 + 1 = 15$

28 $3 + 3 + 1 = 7$

29 $9 + 9 + 1 = 19$

30 $10 + 8$

31 $10 + 5$

32 $10 + 2$

33 $10 + 7$

34 There should be four cars for each child.

35 4

36 4

37 There should be six chocolates for each child.

38 6

39 Circle 5 presents.

40 Circle 3 fish.

Unit 24 MATHS: Measurement & Space

1 Circle truck.

2 Circle teddy.

3 Circle pencil.

4 Draw milk.

5 Draw crayon.

Unit 24 MATHS: Problem Solving

Jaz: fire engine

Zara: dog

Zane: basketball

Tema: Rubik's cube

TERM 3 REVIEW

Term 3 ENGLISH: Grammar & Punctuation

1 children, bicycles

2 boy, lunch

3 girl, city, blocks

4 The lonely scarecrow, the field

5 The red car, the long straight road

6 Wednesday

7 August

8 Miss Vogel

9 Canberra

10 teeth

11 brushes

12 children

13 sticker

14 crabs

15 fish

16 sheep

17 mice

18 foxes

Term 3 ENGLISH: Phonic Knowledge & Spelling

b	l	a	c	k	a	s	c	a	r	e	c	r	o	w
r	z	y	r	q	i	k	j	z	a	k	l	q	w	r
o	t	h	a	r	y	e	t	b	n	o	m	y	l	
w	w	s	b	j	g	l	p	k	f	r	u	i	t	u
n	e	t	t	r	e	e	f	l	l	p	d	o	w	i
x	n	u	h	g	e	t	s	t	o	p	o	n	i	q
a	t	s	d	f	c	o	d	v	w	b	n	m	n	w
z	y	x	s	w	i	n	g	y	e	t	r	c	k	e
q	u	r	p	v	w	u	i	f	r	o	g	o	l	p
r	s	m	i	l	e	d	h	d	f	j	r	k	e	l
e	n	t	d	s	c	f	j	e	g	h	a	c	v	p
u	a	z	e	c	r	a	s	d	z	x	p	b	n	l
t	k	o	r	v	o	g	p	r	e	s	e	n	t	a
y	e	p	a	b	w	n	g	l	a	s	s	b	m	t
d	r	a	g	o	n	m	k	l	a	s	l	i	d	e

Term 3 MATHS: Number & Algebra

1 27, 28, 29, **30**, **31**, 32, 33, **34**, **35**, **36**, 37, **38**, **39**, 40
2 72, 73, 74, **75**, **76**, **77**, 78, **79**, **80**, **81**, **82**, 83, **84**, **85**
3 34, 36, **38**, 40, 42, 44, **46**, **48**, **50**, 52, 54, **56**, **58**, 60
4 5, 10, 15, 20, **25**, **30**, **35**, **40**, 45, **50**, **55**, **60**, **65**, 70
5 10, 20, 30, **40**, **50**, **60**, **70**, 80, **90**, **100**
6 66, 65, 64, 63, **62**, **61**, **60**, 59, **58**, **57**, **56**, 55, **54**, **53**
7 18, 17, 16, **15**, **14**, **13**, **12**, **11**, 10, **9**, **8**, **7**, **6**, **5**

8

5 + 1	8 + 0	3 + 5	7 + 2	2 + 6	3 + 2	5 + 3	4 + 2	7 + 1
■	5 + 3	9 + 1	8 + 2	3 + 7	4 + 6	1 + 9	5 + 1	♥
7 + 0	6 + 1	6 + 4	6 + 3	5 + 2	7 + 1	10 + 0	9 + 0	3 + 6
2 + 1	2 + 7	5 + 5	7 + 3	★	2 + 4	2 + 8	5 + 2	5 + 4
4 + 5	3 + 4	5 + 3	2 + 5	4 + 5	3 + 1	7 + 3	6 + 3	2 + 3
▲	6 + 1	3 + 3	4 + 1	2 + 2	6 + 2	0 + 10	8 + 2	●
6 + 2	4 + 4	6 + 4	5 + 4	0 + 3	2 + 7	5 + 0	6 + 2	4 + 3

9 13
10 19
11 74
12 21
13 35
14 45c
15 $1
16 40c
17 50c
18 B
19 C

Unit 25 ENGLISH: Grammar & Punctuation

1 ran
2 shines
3 eats
4 chased

5 noun
6 verb
7 noun
8 verb
9 verb
10 verb
11 noun
12 verb
13 noun
14 is
15 are
16 am
17 is
18 was
19 were
20–26 Answers will vary. Sample answers provided.
20 is
21 swung
22 sped
23 played
24 is
25 grew
26 lost

Unit 25 ENGLISH: Phonic Knowledge & Spelling

1 all
2 wait
3 late
4 pal
5 but
6 put
7 bug
8 pup
9 rope
10 pot
11 not
12 robe
13 meet
14 end
15 wet
16 teeth
17 bit
18 ripe
19 sing
20 trip

Unit 25 ENGLISH: Reading & Comprehension

1 c. a poem
2 b. a guinea pig
3 a. little
4 b. false
5 b. Run away.
6 squeak
7 c. The guinea pig knew a mouse was not a rat.
8 big
9 told
10 a. It died.

ANSWERS

TARGETING HOMEWORK 1 © PASCAL PRESS ISBN 9781925726435

Unit 26 MATHS: Number & Algebra

1 3 tens and 4 ones = 34
    30 + 4 = 34
    10 + 10 + 10 + 4 = 34
    10 + 10 + 14 = 34
2 7 tens and 9 ones = 79
    70 + 9 = 79
    10 + 10 + 59 = 79
    60 + 10 + 9 = 79
    50 + 10 + 19 = 79
3 4 tens and 7 ones = 47
4 3 tens and 5 ones = 35
5 10, 20, 30, 40, 50, 60, 70, 80, 90, 100
6 3
7 5
8 3

Unit 26 MATHS: Measurement & Space

1 cube
2 sphere
3 cone
4 cylinder
5 rectangular prism
6 cone
7 sphere
8 rectangular prism
9 cube
10 cylinder
11 first glass
12 fifth glass
13 third glass
14 second glass
15 fourth glass

Unit 26 MATHS: Problem Solving

Sam's glass is half full.
Tema's glass is less than half full.
Sasha's glass is more than half full.

Unit 27 ENGLISH: Grammar & Punctuation

1 walks
2 ride
3 does
4 swim
5 runs
6 dances
7 jump
8 will wait
9 will play
10 blew
11 took
12 wrote

Unit 27 ENGLISH: Phonic Knowledge & Spelling

1 sheep
2 call
3 eight
4 bit
5 splat
6 man

7 puppy
8 grape
9 eight
10 set
11 pool
12 gone

Unit 27 ENGLISH: Reading & Comprehension

1 a. Ash
2 c. Ash's cousin Sarah
3 b. at school
4 b. at lunch
5 c. nice
6 c. Some big kids were being mean to him.
7 a. to help him
8 b. upset
9 a. worried
10 Answers will vary; e.g. tell the teacher, tell her parents.

Unit 28 MATHS: Number & Algebra

1 7 tens and 6 ones = 76
2 9 tens and 9 ones = 99
3 10, 20, 30, 40, 50, 60, 70, 80, 90, 100
4 100 + 3 = 103
5 100 + 6 = 106
6 96, 98, 99, 102, 103, 105
7 3
8 5
9 6
10 5

Unit 28 MATHS: Measurement & Space

1 2 o'clock
2 6 o'clock
3 5 o'clock
4 half past 9
5 half past 4
6 half past 7
7 half past 3

8 half past 10

9 half past 8

10 tree
11 bone
12 treasure chest

Unit 28 MATHS: Problem Solving

1 15
2 11
3 Start at the star. Go up 7. Go left 4.

Unit 29 ENGLISH: Grammar & Punctuation

1 big
2 yellow
3 funny
4 tiny
5 Three
6 happy
7 huge
8 each
9 tasty
10 late
11 red
12 fast
13 broken
14 enormous
15 excited

Unit 29 ENGLISH: Phonic Knowledge & Spelling

1 p<u>o</u>t 1
2 p<u>u</u>mp<u>ki</u>n 2
3 s<u>u</u>per 2
4 tom<u>a</u>t<u>o</u> 3
5 cr<u>o</u>c<u>o</u>d<u>i</u>le 3
6 c<u>a</u>ne 1
7 h<u>a</u>mm<u>e</u>r 2
8 h<u>a</u>pp<u>y</u> 2
9 str<u>a</u>wberr<u>y</u> 3
10 s<u>u</u>perm<u>a</u>rk<u>e</u>t 4
11 hun + dred
12 pic + nic
13 but + ter
14 roc + ket
15 bed + room
16 sor + ry
17 ap + ple
18 kit + ten
19 buc + ket

Unit 29 ENGLISH: Reading & Comprehension

1 b. to the beach
2 a. a sandcastle
3 c. up near the dunes
4 b. shells
5 a. a crab
6 c. amused
7 Nala and Jack
8 Nala
9 a. So it wouldn't wash away.
10 Answers will vary; e.g. seaweed.

Unit 30 MATHS: Number & Algebra

1 101, 102, 103, 104, 106, 107, 108, 109
2 104, 106, 108, 114, 116
3 110, 115, 130, 135, 140
4 70, 80, 90, 130, 140
5 100 + 10 + 3 = 113
6 100 + 10 + 7 = 117
7 6 − 3 = 3
8 12 − 6 = 6
9 8 − 5 = 3
10 7 + 3 = 10

11 45c
12 50c
13 50c
14 $3
15 paints
16 dog
17 trophy
18 ball
19 dog

Unit 30 MATHS: Statistics

1

2 yellow
3 4
4 green
5 28
6 yellow
7 2
8 5
9 red
10 1

Unit 30 MATHS: Problem Solving

3	1	2	4
2	4	3	1
1	3	4	2
4	2	1	3

1	3	4	2
4	2	1	3
3	4	2	1
2	1	3	4

Unit 31 ENGLISH: Grammar & Punctuation

1 tiny
2 few
3 right
4 wrong
5 last
6 sick
7 slow
8 tall
9 cold
10 unlucky, not lucky
11 unkind, not kind
12 unafraid, not afraid

TARGETING HOMEWORK 1 © PASCAL PRESS ISBN 9781925726435

13 unfair, not fair

14 unwell, not well

15 untidy, not tidy

16 unsafe, not safe

17 unhealthy, not healthy

18 unused, not used

Unit 31 ENGLISH: Phonic Knowledge & Spelling

1 butter + fly

2 cup + cake

3 rail + road

4 rainbow

5 pancake

6 eyeball

7 mousetrap

8 campfire

9 birthday

10 earthworm

11 sunshine

12 airport

13 football

14 popcorn

Unit 31 ENGLISH: Reading & Comprehension

1 a. Little Koala

2 b. Snake

3 her family

4 3

5 Echidna family

6 Saturday

7 b. 2 pm

8 c. gumnut crackers

9 b. bush punch

10 b. 21

Unit 32 MATHS: Number & Algebra

1 1 hundred, 1 ten and 3 ones = 113

2 1 hundred, 1 ten and 1 one = 111

3 1 hundred, 1 ten and 4 ones = 114

4 1 hundred, 0 tens and 7 ones = 107

5 1 hundred, 1 ten and 0 ones = 110

6 1 hundred, 2 tens and 4 ones = 124

7 0 hundreds, 7 tens and 2 ones = 72

8 1 hundred, 0 tens and 0 ones = 100

9 86

10 115

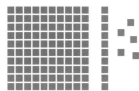

11 109

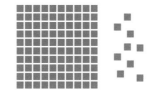

12 121

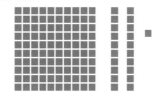

13 25, 30, 35, 40, 45, 50, 55, 60, 65. Counting in 5s.

14 75, 80, 85, 90, 95, 100, 105, 110. Counting in 5s.

15 100, 102, 104, 106, 108, 110, 112, 114. Counting in 2s.

16 70, 80, 90, 100, 110, 120, 130, 140. Counting in 10s.

17 98, 99, 100, 101, 102, 103, 104, 105. Counting in 1s.

18 106, 105, 104, 103, 102, 101, 100, 99. Counting in 1s.

19 50 + 40 = 90

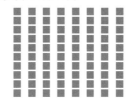

20 40 + 30 = 70

21 Circle 3 groups of 5

22 15

23 5

24 3

25 Circle 6 groups of 2

26 12

27 2

28 6

29 Circle 3 groups of 4

30 12

31 4

32 3

33 18

34 6

35 3

36 Repeat: ▲ ▲ ▲   Draw: ▲ ▲

37 Repeat: dog, cat, pig, dog   Write: dog, dog

38 Repeat: 1, 1, 2   Write: 2, 1

Unit 32 MATHS: Problem Solving

4	9	2
3	5	7
8	1	6

ANSWERS

Term 4 ENGLISH: Grammar & Punctuation

1 gallop
2 swim
3 slither
4 jump
5 eat
6 squawk
7 stops
8 are
9 am
10 will ask
11 rode
12 busy
13 unhappy
14 untidy
15 first
16 five
17 scary
18 funny
19 dirty
20 shady

Term 4 ENGLISH: Phonic Knowledge & Spelling

1 wash
2 come
3 bit
4 rid
5 gone
6 put
7 met
8 mat
9 night
10 belt
11 ga_llop, 2, gal + lop
12 fli_pper, 2, flip + per
13 bu_tter, 2, but + ter
14 ha_ppy, 2, hap + py
15 chi_cken, 2, chic + ken
16 footprint
17 sunshine
18 birthday
19 breakfast
20 skateboard

Term 4 MATHS: Number & Algebra

1 1 hundred, 0 tens and 3 ones = 103
2 1 hundred, 1 ten and 0 ones = 110
3 1 hundred, 1 ten and 6 ones = 116
4 0 hundreds, 5 tens and 2 ones = 52
5 96, 98, 100, 102, 104, 106, 108, 110. Counting in 2s.
6 85, 90, 95, 100, 105, 110, 115, 120. Counting in 5s.
7 73, 75, 77, 79, 81, 83, 85, 87. Counting in 2s.
8 70, 80, 90, 100, 110, 120, 130, 140. Counting in 10s.
9 99, 100, 101, 102, 103, 104, 105, 106. Counting in 1s.
10 $9 - 5 = 4$
11 $8 - 3 = 4$
12 $12 - 4 = 8$
13 $4 + 5 = 9$

Term 4 MATHS: Measurement & Space

1 half past 10
2 4 o'clock
3 6 o'clock
4 half past 1

TARGETING HOMEWORK 1 © PASCAL PRESS ISBN 9781925726435